THEODORE ROOSEVELT
AND HIS AMERICA

Milton Meltzer

THEODORE ROOSEVELT

★ AND HIS AMERICA ★

FRANKLIN WATTS
A Division of Grolier Publishing
New York / London / Hong Kong / Sydney
Danbury, Connecticut

Picture research by Mary Ellen Casey

Photographs copyright ©: Brown Brothers, Sterling, Pa.: p. 2; The Bettmann
Archive: pp. 75, 79, 84, 85, 93, 133, 140; all other photographs copyright © Theodore
Roosevelt Collection, Houghton Library, Harvard University.

Library of Congress Cataloging-in-Publication Data
Meltzer, Milton, 1915–
Theodore Roosevelt and his America / Milton Meltzer.
p.   cm.
Includes bibliographical references and index.
ISBN 0-531-11192-X
1. Roosevelt, Theodore, 1858–1919.   2. Presidents—United States—
Biography.   3. United States—Politics and government—1865–1933.
I. Title.
E757.M49   1994
973.91'1'092—dc20
[B]   94-17369   CIP   AC

CONTENTS

FOREWORD

This is the fifth time I've chosen to write the biography of a U.S. president. Before Theodore Roosevelt, there were Washington, Jefferson, Jackson, and Lincoln. Why, again, a president? Perhaps because presidents sit in a position of such tremendous power. Well, potential power, at least, for some have made feeble use of their high office. (Others have misused it, stretching the power well beyond its constitutional limits.)

But power to do what? To carry out the wishes of the people? To meet the crises and emergencies that sometimes so unpredictably strike a nation with terrible force? I mean foreign wars, civil wars, great depressions, plagues, violent clashing of contending parties or classes. . . . Sometimes a president may serve his country best by not going along with the popular vote. For the majority does not always vote for what's best, even to satisfy their own needs. They may be swept away by blind passion or prejudice, and it is then that a great president must awaken them to their peril and try to turn them in a better, saner direction. Of course a president may also play deliberately to passion and prejudice, even creating or intensifying them, for his own selfish political advantage.

This time, I chose Theodore Roosevelt as my subject because he lived in a time of great change (1858–1919). And his years in the White House (1901–1909) came at the opening of the twentieth century. The modern age began with his presidency. It was a period of rapid industrialization, of the building of great financial empires, of the drive for colonial expansion. Theodore Roosevelt had strong opinions about those changes and didn't hesitate to act on them.

As a little boy he showed great interest in and love for the natural world, an intense feeling that later led him to pioneer, as president, efforts to preserve great tracts of the American wilderness for the public's enjoyment.

"Joy in life"—that phrase characterizes him again and again in the memoirs of friends. Theodore Roosevelt loved to hunt, camp, travel, ranch, play politics, and fight wars. But the greatest joy in his life came when he succeeded to the presidency.

This book is about his path to the presidency, and what he did with the power that was placed in his hands.

1

AN ARISTOCRAT'S BEGINNINGS

Theodore Roosevelt was born rich, into a family that had been in America since the 1600s. TR (we'll call him that for short; he had too many nicknames to keep track of) grew up to become the twenty-sixth president of the United States.

He was one of the most popular we've ever had. But "popular" doesn't necessarily mean "best." People can sometimes love a president for the wrong reasons. His personality, for instance—charming, clever, enjoys his job and living in the White House so much it makes the voters feel good.

That's how most Americans felt about TR. Just how good a president was he? Well, compared to whom? And by what standards? Let's try to find out by looking at what he did, why he did it, and what the result was. But to understand who the man was, we need to go back to his beginnings.

Roosevelt. That's the name TR inherited. Originally the name was Rosenvelt, after the town in the Netherlands that the family came from. (In Dutch the word means "field of roses.") The first Roosevelt to reach these shores was one of the early Dutch settlers in New Amsterdam.

There were only about one hundred houses on the lower tip of Manhattan when he arrived. TR was of the seventh generation to be born on the island of Manhattan. The Roosevelts began their American life as farmers, but gradually moved up the social ladder, through manufacturing, trading, engineering, and banking, all the while piling up more wealth.

By the time TR was born—on October 27, 1858—his grandpa Roosevelt was worth half a million dollars. A huge sum, when you realize that in those days the average worker earned about fifty cents a day. TR's folks lived in a brownstone at 28 East Twentieth Street, with a garden behind it. (You can visit the house now; it's a national historic site, open to the public.) "Sweet and pretty" was his grandma's verdict on the newborn. Noisy, too! (He always would be.) But sickly from the start. The infant suffered from asthma; it was only the first of many ailments that would plague him.

By contrast, Theodore Roosevelt, Sr., was a healthy, robust man, busily increasing the family fortune by dealing in plate glass and real estate. But he gave much time to helping others less fortunate than he. He was a founder of the Children's Aid Society, taught Sunday school every week, and did much charitable work for children of the poor. He was a founder of the Metropolitan Museum of Art and of the American Museum of Natural History. He had a powerful drive to get things done, and get them done right. (In this his son would be much like him.) Yet he enjoyed life to the full—horseback riding in Central Park, dancing at society balls, playing with his children. (TR was his second child and first son.)

Mrs. Roosevelt—she had been Martha Bulloch, the beautiful belle of a Georgia plantation—liked fine paintings, furniture, porcelain, and wines, and filled the house with them. When the Civil War began, not long after TR's birth, his mother was fiercely loyal to the Confederate cause and the slaveholding society she was raised in. Two of her brothers fought for the South. TR's father, a Lincoln man, unable to go against his wife and his brothers-in-law, did what many rich northerners did: he paid for a substitute to fight in his place.

But, his conscience troubling him, he found a way to aid the Union cause as a civilian. He spent months in Washington, working hard to get Congress to pass a bill that he himself wrote, which would provide for soldiers to set aside voluntary

A drawing of the building where Teddy Roosevelt was born. The house at 28 East Twentieth Street, in New York City, has since been reconstructed and is now open to visitors.

Theodore Roosevelt, Sr., was a philanthropist who contributed to the founding of the Metropolitan Museum of Art, the American Museum of Natural History, and the Children's Aid Society. Although a strict disciplinarian, he was a kind father, encouraging his son's pursuits in the natural sciences. TR's mother, Martha Bulloch Roosevelt, a Southerner by birth, often read poetry and folktales to her children.

This is the first photo of Teddy Roosevelt, taken shortly before he turned two.

contributions from their pay to be sent home to their families. After its passage, TR's father rode from camp to camp to urge the soldiers to take advantage of the plan. It proved of great benefit to families where money was badly needed.

Yet TR seems to have been ashamed of his father's failure to put on a uniform and fight, which at the time was considered the right and manly thing to do. Years later, in his autobiography, he never mentioned his father's role in the Civil War. And as though to make up for his father's not fighting, he always showed a passionate desire to fight and shed blood himself.

During the father's long wartime absences from home, Mrs. Roosevelt had charge of the children. There were four now: Anna, the eldest, then TR, Elliott, and, finally, Corinne. Strangely, since they had such healthy parents, the children were a sickly lot. Anna had been dropped as a baby and had to wear a harness to correct the spinal defect caused by the fall. TR was almost always sick: colds, coughs, nausea, fevers, diarrhea, and the asthma that got so bad that he had to sleep propped up in bed or in a big chair. Elliott was subject to "nervous attacks," and Corinne, too, would soon start to suffer from asthma.

Mrs. Roosevelt adored her family, but she barely managed even the limited duties expected of her in a house full of servants. She was helped by her unmarried sister, Anna Bulloch, who came up from Georgia to live in the Roosevelt home. Making a classroom of the second-floor nursery, Mrs. Roosevelt taught the children the three Rs—reading, writing, and arithmetic. With her soft southern drawl and her acting skills, she got them to love the Brer Rabbit tales, the poems of Longfellow, and stories from the magazine *Our Young Folks*. For facts and moral values they waded through the pages of the McGuffey readers.

TR loved to hear about the adventures on the frontier of Daniel Boone and Davy Crockett and the bravery of the Bullochs fighting during the American Revolution. Early on, his taste favored legendary heroes and their dramatic exploits. He could never read enough to satisfy his thirst for information. One of his favorite books, even before he could read, was a massive illustrated volume of missionary travels in Africa. The pictures of wild animals roaming the land or being hunted in the great rivers and mountains of that remote continent thrilled him, and he would beg the grown-ups to tell him the stories behind the pictures. In the family library, as he learned to read, he found books on natural history. They seemed to kindle an inborn love for the phenomena of the natural world. He would curl up in his favorite little red upholstered chair and examine these books endlessly.

The child's mind prickled with curiosity—ever alert to the new and challenging. But his body kept failing. Would he be an invalid for life? Restless at steady confinement to the house, he would act up and make a pest of himself. Once he bit his elder sister on the arm and, knowing it was wrong, hid under the kitchen table. His father dragged him out and whacked him. It was the only time he punished his son physically; it never proved necessary again. Tell a lie, act selfish, be cruel or cowardly, and you knew Papa would react swiftly. TR Senior's aim was to make his children obey his very first order, something his wife was rarely able to do. But both agreed that "the same standard of clean living was demanded for the boys as for the girls; that what was wrong in a woman could not be right in a man."

TR's interest in nature expanded when the family vacationed for a few summers at a country place in New Jersey. Still weakened by the constant asthma attacks, TR drew on a store of nervous energy to wander in the woods, gather nuts and apples, hunt frogs, and help to bring in the hay. Unlike the other children, he observed the natural life around him with great care. He studied the birds, noted their calls, checked what he had learned from books against what he could see for himself, and squirreled it all away in his memory.

By seven, the seeds of a naturalist's career planted so early in him were ready to bear fruit. He tells how:

★

Teddy at age five

I was walking up Broadway, and as I passed the market to which I used sometimes to be sent before breakfast to get strawberries, I suddenly saw a dead seal laid out on a slab of wood. That seal filled me with every possible feeling of romance and adventure. I asked where it was killed, and was informed in the harbor. . . . As long as that seal remained there I haunted the neighborhood of the market day after day. I measured it, and I recall that, not having a tape measure, I had to do my best to get its girth with a folding pocket foot-rule, a difficult undertaking. I carefully made a record of the utterly useless measurements, and at once began to write a natural history of my own, on the strength of that seal. This, and subsequent natural histories, were written down in blank books in simplified spelling, wholly unpremeditated and unscientific. I had vague aspirations of in some way or another owning that seal, but they never got beyond the purely formless stage. I think, however, I did get the seal's skull, and with two of my cousins promptly started what we ambitiously called the "Roosevelt Museum of Natural History."

Two years later, at nine, he wrote his first scientific paper— "Natural History on Insects," he called it. In it he solemnly declared that all the insects in this book lived in North America, and while a friend had given him some facts, mostly he learned about the insects' habits from observation. He took up spiders, ants, ladybugs, fireflies, beetles, dragonflies, and, breaking his framework, threw in facts about hawks, minnows, and crayfish. Young as he was, he managed to arrange the classification of insects methodically and to index them properly.

Evidence of young TR's fascination with living things might crop up most unexpectedly. Once, he met a friend of the family on a streetcar and politely lifted his hat to her, whereupon "several frogs leaped gaily to the floor." Guests in the home learned to watch where they sat lest they crush some helpless creature. Snakes might be found in water pitchers,

Early in his life, Teddy Roosevelt became fascinated by nature. Some days he spent long hours observing animals and collecting interesting specimens; eventually he made detailed drawings of individual species.

field mice in the icebox, and snapping turtles in the kitchen sink. Once, a disgusting smell pervaded the house because TR had ordered the cook to boil an animal, fur and all, for twenty-four hours so he could study its anatomy. When his parents were going away, he always pressed them to bring home "curiosities and living things."

When TR was nine the family took a summer place up along the Hudson River. TR began to keep a diary. It's full of the pleasures of swimming, hiking, and riding a pony every day for six miles before breakfast. Yet when the summer of 1868 ended, TR's father worried that this active boy was getting no better. He was terribly thin and pale. And Mrs. Roosevelt's health worried him, too. Since the end of the Civil War, lamenting all the death and destruction in her defeated Georgia, she had declined into invalidism. She gave up even attempting to run the household, and the children began to treat her like a helpless family pet.

So when Mrs. Roosevelt suggested that a long trip to Europe might be good for the whole family, Mr. Roosevelt agreed. He could easily take leave from a thriving business. And, from a grand tour of Europe, the children would learn a good deal of value. (None of them had had any schooling but from Aunt Annie.)

They left New York in May 1869 and were gone a whole year. For months the children had prepared by studying travel books and tracing routes on maps. But they didn't look forward to the tour. They hated to leave their friends and familiar surroundings. TR cried over being separated from his favorite friend, Edith Carow. Edith often played in their home and had shared Aunt Annie's classes. TR and Edith exchanged letters that reveal how bored TR was and how much he missed his Edie. He signed his letters, "Ever your loving friend, T. Roosevelt." Her letters, too, show how lonely she was for him.

All through the European tour Mr. Roosevelt worried over TR's poor health. Vicious attacks of asthma laid the boy low again and again. Yet he was never self-pitying. Several times the boy was taken to doctors. Nothing prescribed had any effect. When at last, in May 1870, their ship entered the home port, TR shouted, "New York! Hip! Hurrah!"

Happy to be home, yet no healthier. Worse, if anything. Nearly twelve now, TR had grown tall for his age, but he stayed skinny. Standing on his pipe-stem legs he looked like a young stork. His blond hair was rarely combed. His blue eyes, extremely nearsighted since birth, never rested, for he read constantly. And he talked constantly. Often he sought out older people to conduct long conversations with them, usually on natural history.

That fall the family doctor gave TR a thorough examination. The doctor urged exercise that would develop the boy's chest, so that his lungs, weakened by asthma, would have room to expand, making the act of breathing less of a strain on his heart. Theodore Senior, deeply troubled by his son's frailty, decided something drastic had to be done. He called in TR and said, "You have the mind, but you have not the body, and without the help of the body the mind cannot go as far as it should. You must *make* the body." And as the story goes, the boy replied, *"I'll make the body."* That was the first time the boy took on a responsibility.

Mr. Roosevelt converted the back bedroom on the second floor to an open-air porch, putting in gymnasium equipment. Here, all the children worked out daily to build up their bodies on parallel bars and ladders.

TR spent many long hours, too, at the punching bag and with the dumbbells. Gradually his chest expanded and his muscles hardened.

Still, he resented the time spent on physical exercise. Until one day he was shamed by an encounter with four boys his own age. He was alone when they came up and began to tease him. At first he took it, then decided to fight. But each of the boys, laughing at his weakness, was able to hold him off at arm's length. TR wasn't hurt, but deeply humiliated. He came home and began boxing lessons and taking his workouts more seriously. By his teens he was chalking up victories in the dashes, the broad jump, and the pole vault.

No longer was his diary peppered with sad notes on bouts of illness. His interest in nature grew even more intense. He began identifying by their scientific names the specimens he observed. And he collected hundreds more to add to his private museum. During the summer, he got neighborhood boys to help him collect by offering them ten cents for each field mouse and thirty-five cents for each family of mice. They soon realized he wanted just about any creature that could swim, fly, run, or crawl.

Private tutors replaced his aunt. They taught him French, German, and Latin while they improved his English (though he never could master spelling). An old expert taught him taxidermy—the art of preparing, stuffing, and mounting the skins of animals in lifelike form. Soon he could preserve the specimens he caught. When he was fourteen his father bought him his first gun. But when he took it out to hunt, he was startled to find he missed everything. That was how he learned how bad his eyesight was, and he began to wear his first pair of eyeglasses. "I had no idea how beautiful the world was until I got those spectacles," he said.

In October 1872, the family left home on another foreign tour. This time the goal was Egypt and the Holy Land. TR again hated to leave his friends, but if he could turn this into a scientific expedition, it wouldn't be so bad. With his new spectacles he could see much better and record far more in his notebooks.

Now in his early teens, he was an odd-looking boy. Big spectacles, big buck teeth bared in a wide grin, hair dirty blond and down over his collar, bony wrists and ankles, and a harsh, shrill voice. His fingers were always stained with ink and chemicals.

After passing through England and Europe, the family soon reached Egypt, "the land of my dreams," said TR. There he noted in his diary a vast variety of birds strange to him— their looks, their sounds, their movements. To his father it seemed certain TR would become a professional naturalist, a decent career if not an especially profitable one. What else could he do? He would never be successful in commerce or industry, and his physical condition barred him from a military career.

Cruising on the Nile, TR shot his first bird, a warbler, and, excited by this success, killed over a hundred more before the voyage ended. Now his father delighted him with the gift of a double-barreled shotgun. After he shot a bird, he prepared its skin, a procedure requiring some twenty-five steps. The largest bird he killed was a crane. "I never enjoyed myself so much," he wrote to an aunt.

After visiting Palestine and Syria, the Roosevelts traveled on to Greece. In April 1873, TR and his brother Elliott were placed with a German family in Dresden. They would spend the next five months studying German. His father left for home, and the rest of the family dispersed throughout Europe. The boys worked hard at mastering the language—"harder than I have ever studied before in my life," said TR. He was even able to translate into English difficult German texts of natural history.

With humor he reported to his mother a new development, linking it to his love for animals: "Picture to yourself an antiquated woodchuck with his cheecks [sic] filled with nuts, his face well oiled, his voice hoarse from gargling and a cloth resembling in texture and cleanliness a secondhand dustman's castoff stocking around his head, picture to yourself that, I say, and you will have a good likeness of your hopeful offspring while suffering from an attack of the mumps."

Still, he concentrated on his studies and set the pace for Elliott. By the time the boys left Dresden to rejoin the family, Fraulein Anna Minkwitz, TR's German tutor, told Mrs. Roosevelt that she need not be anxious about TR: "He will surely one day be a great professor, or who knows, he may become even President of the United States."

2

THE HARVARD MAN

In November 1873 the Roosevelts were back in New York. But this time to live in their new town house at 6 West Fifty-seventh Street, just off Fifth Avenue. It had been prepared for them in their absence. It was big, grander than the Twentieth Street home, and furnished elegantly. It had a fully equipped gymnasium on the top floor and space in the garret for TR's museum of natural history.

To his friends TR looked different now—taller, more serious, and, yes, something of a prude. He detested boys who swore or told dirty jokes. However, he was just as strong-willed and cocky as before. A cousin remarked that TR was still sure that "he could do things better than anyone else."

His parents felt the fifteen-year-old was ready to take on a second major responsibility. His health had vastly improved. Now he must prepare himself for college. They wanted him to enter Harvard in the fall of 1876. That gave him less than three years to study for the necessary examinations. With his love of reading, his travels abroad, and his skill in languages, he had a good start. But his formal education had been spotty. So he was sent to Arthur Cutler for tutoring. Studying eight hours a day, TR covered three years of work in two. Even while vacationing at the family's new summer place at Oyster Bay, on the north shore of Long Island, he kept up his studies. He passed his entrance exams with no trouble.

The three summers TR would spend at Oyster Bay before entering college were joyous—and busy. Many visitors came—cousins, friends, and, of course, Edith Carow. They went swimming, boating, horseback riding, and hiking. TR kept up his bodybuilding exercises. At seventeen he weighed 124 pounds and stood 5 feet 8 inches tall. He had grown side-whiskers now, and, although he was not handsome, his whole personality radiated gaiety.

On his field trips around Oyster Bay, he noted many shore and maritime birds, most of which he had never seen before. He kept track of the times of arrival and departure of the migrating birds and recorded their habitats. Strangely, he never commented on their visual beauty—their color, their plumage—though he took great pains to describe their songs in words.

He made some trips to the Adirondacks, hiring Mose Sawyer as guide. Mose recalled long after that TR was a good camper who never smoked, drank, or cussed. He always did his share of camp chores. He didn't fish and was interested only in shooting, skinning, and mounting birds. "A queer looker," said Mose, "but smart."

TR's friendship with Edith deepened. They spent long hours together, reading aloud to each other, sharing confidences. It seemed to some that the two had reached an understanding. As if to claim her, he painted her name on the stern of his rowboat.

In September 1876, TR left for Cambridge, Massachusetts, to begin his studies at Harvard. It was a small provincial college then, its 800 students drawn from the elite class. Most came from Boston or nearby, had gone to the fashionable prep schools of New England, and limited their friends to their own social set. In TR's freshman class of some 250 there were no Jews, no Boston Irish, no African-Americans, no foreigners. Even to have come from New York, aristocrat though you might be, made you something of an outsider.

The classic student pose was boredom. You couldn't be seen as concerned with anything intellectual. Indeed, Henry Adams, who had recently taught history at Harvard, said his students were "ignorant of all that man had ever thought and hoped."

TR at age seventeen, standing at the left. His brother Elliott is on the right, his sister Corinne is in the center, and their friend Edith Carow is seated on the ground.

Harvard occupied only a few redbrick buildings in TR's time. They were scattered about the elms in the Yard, which was enclosed by a low fence. Towering over all were the ramparts of the newly finished Memorial Hall. Unlike most of the students, TR did not live in the dormitories. His parents had feared the damp ground-floor rooms assigned to freshmen would harm their son's health. His elder sister had come down earlier to take a second floor room for him at 16 Winthrop Street, off Harvard Square. He settled in comfortably among his collection of stuffed birds and his books, with his mother's photograph smiling down from the mantel above the fireplace.

Harvard habits contrasted sharply with TR's. The students drank a lot; TR almost never did. Gentlemen should never hurry; a leisurely walk was the way to get about. TR was always rushing around. Athletics; what other subject was there to talk about? But TR liked to argue ideas. So much so that he couldn't shut up. In class he often interrupted lecturers with questions, to the point where one annoyed professor cried out, "Now look here, Roosevelt, let me talk! I'm running this course!"

TR didn't make a lot of friends. Closest to him was Henry Minot, who shared his passion for birds. TR kept in constant touch by mail with his family back in New York. His letters express his love for them and his awareness of how much he owed them. To his mother he once wrote that "I have never spent an unhappy day unless by my own fault." And to his father he confided, "I do not think there is a fellow in College who has a family who love him as much as you all do me. . . . I am sure that there is no one who has a Father who is also his best and most intimate friend, as you are mine."

As TR began his studies, Harvard was undergoing major changes that would lift it to the topmost rank of American universities. The new president, Charles W. Eliot, had collected a superb group of scholars in several fields and given upperclassmen the freedom to choose courses they preferred. Only first-year students were not allowed electives. TR had to take mathematics, physics, chemistry, classical literature,

Greek, Latin, and German. He did reasonably well in most courses, for he had trained himself to carry out strict routines. He averaged 75 when 50 was the passing grade.

In later years, however, looking back at what Harvard taught him, he regretted that the college stressed individualism rather than the need for cooperation. He thought the students were given no sense of obligation "to join with others in trying to make things better for the many by curbing the abnormal and excessive development of individualism in a few."

Despite the burden of so many courses, TR still found time for fun. He worked out in the college gym, rowed on the Charles River, organized a club to play whist, a card game, and taught a Sunday school class. He plunged into the social life, going to dinner parties, the theater, and dances. He met many girls, but none he thought as lovely as Edith Carow, who visited him in Cambridge. Always he was "rigidly virtuous." Sex was for marriage only, he believed, and pleasurable though it might be, its purpose was to procreate.

At Harvard he enjoyed the company of the rich, the fashionable, and the snobbish. He soon quit taking his meals in the Commons and joined an exclusive student eating club, checking on the social credentials of new acqaintances to make sure they would make suitable friends. Overly concerned with social rank, he ignored almost everyone he considered beneath him.

With his Dutch name and his odd manner it took a while for TR to win acceptance among the elite. But his wide enthusiasm, his bumptious energy, and his happy nature were irresistible. TR is "crazy," or "eccentric," they might say, but never, surely, dull.

On his first summer vacation from college TR explored the shores of Adirondack lakes. Returning to Oyster Bay, he published a four-page pamphlet listing ninety-seven different species of summer birds that had been seen in one of the mountain counties. It was the first of many publications.

As TR's sophomore year at Harvard drew near, his father told him he must make his own way in the world. If he meant to do scientific research, then he must do it seriously. Mr. Roosevelt assured his son that the family had enough money to permit relatively low-paying work, as long as TR would do the very best he was capable of. He did not want his son to dabble in science like a dilettante. "After this conversation," TR recalled later, "I fully intended to make science my life-work."

Back in Cambridge, TR could now choose some of his courses. He elected botany and anatomy, both taught by the distinguished William James, and also French and German. These were in addition to three required courses. Again he took care of his health by boxing and wrestling. He wrote for the *Advocate*, the college magazine, and was invited to join one of the exclusive clubs. That fall he made his first political gesture, marching in a torchlight parade for Rutherford B. Hayes, the Republican presidential candidate in the 1876 election.

In mid-December came disturbing news: Mr. Roosevelt was not well. TR wrote to beg him to take it easy. But a few days later his father collapsed. He had cancer of the stomach. When TR came home for Christmas, his father seemed somewhat better. But in January his condition worsened rapidly. With TR preparing for the midyear exams, the family decided not to tell him how bad things were. Then came a telegram asking TR to rush home. He arrived the next morning only to find his beloved father had died some hours before, at the age of forty-seven.

For months TR was overcome with grief. The sense of loss was crippling. He tried to act cheerful on campus, but could not shake his melancholy. Finally he plunged into his studies, resolved that hard work was what his father expected of him. And when the sophomore year ended, he had raised his average to 89, winning honors in six of his eight courses.

His father had left him about $125,000, a large inheritance that ensured a comfortable life. TR spent the summer at Oyster Bay, riding, rowing, swimming, sailing in fair or foul weather. Everything about the house reminded him of his father. He took comfort from the August visit of Edith Carow. Day after day they went riding, rowing, or sailing. But then, late in her visit, they had a falling-out. No one knows why. TR's diary is blank for those days. Some speculate that he asked her to marry him and she refused. Others say that shortly before his death, Mr. Roosevelt had discouraged such a match because he disapproved of Edith's father, an alcoholic. Edith never explained the break herself, except to say that TR had "not been nice."

Whatever the reason, the rupture upset TR badly. Again he buried his disappointment with violent physical exercise and by going off to the Maine woods for three weeks. He was out in the wilderness in all kinds of weather, guided by Bill Sewall, a six-footer, thirty-three years old, who didn't smoke or drink, and who read his Bible daily, and recited poetry while paddling their canoe. The older man found the college boy different from anyone he'd ever met—"fairminded," a lad who "took pains to learn everything. . . . He was quick to find the real man in very simple men." TR, in turn, was taken with Sewall, perhaps seeing another father in him, and a warm friendship grew between them.

In his junior year TR studied zoology, geology, German, Italian, and political economy. He was a member of several clubs—the Rifle, the Natural History, the Finance, and was initiated into the snobbiest of all, the Porcellian. "My best friends are in it," he wrote home. They included Dick Saltonstall, whose home in Chestnut Hill he often visited. It was there on an October weekend in 1878, that he met Alice Hathaway Lee.

It was love at first sight.

3

LOVE AT FIRST SIGHT

Alice Lee was the cousin of TR's friend, Dick Saltonstall. She, too, lived in Chestnut Hill, Brookline, a six-mile buggy ride from Harvard Square. "I think her one of the sweetest and most ladylike girls I have ever met," TR wrote in his diary. By the end of that weekend in her company, he vowed he would marry her.

Alice was seventeen when she met the nineteen-year-old college junior. She was a willowy blonde, almost TR's height. People said she was "enchanting," "endearing," "the life of the party." So carried away was TR that he wrote, "I had never before cared a snap of my finger for any girl." (How quickly did he drive Edith Carow from his mind!) Lovely Alice, born to wealth and privilege, was the center of young men's attention. But how very dull they were, compared to TR! Yet his very strangeness made her nervous—his clothes smelling faintly of arsenic, his stained fingers, his shrill chattering voice, his curly whiskers, his gleaming glasses, his prominent teeth, his passion for collecting bugs and birds. But who else was so bright, so fascinating, so ardent?

The courtship began, with Alice making him welcome to her home, yet not committing herself to more than friendship. While she dominated his thoughts, he did not neglect his studies. He prepared papers for the Natural History Society on such topics as crustaceans and birds, and even made his first public speech at the annual dinner of the *Harvard Crimson,* the college newspaper. From this stammering effort no one could have guessed he would one day talk before more audiences than any other orator of his time.

Ahead was the prospect of going, after four years at Harvard, to some university in Europe, there to spend three more years earning a doctoral degree. Yes, it was necessary for a career in science. But did he really want to give the rest of his life to science? No one had encouraged him in that pursuit—neither his professors at Harvard nor his family. And how would a long absence affect his courtship of Alice? She had made it plain she did not like that messy business of killing and stuffing animals, nor did marriage to a professor or doctor appeal to her. TR began to think politics might be a better choice, and even asked one of his professors what he thought. The answer: government is much more in need of idealistic young men than are scientific laboratories.

In the late spring of 1879, as the school year was ending, TR asked Alice to marry him. No, she said, but it was clear he was welcome to pursue his courtship come fall. When TR's grades for his junior year came in, they showed he had led everyone in both zoology and political economy, and he made his choice: he would give up all thought of becoming a scientist. It would be politics from now on.

The summer passed with the usual pleasures at Oyster Bay and another trip to Maine, where he and Bill Sewall climbed its highest peak, Mount Katahdin. Then they took a 50-mile, six-day canoe expedition up the Aroostook River, followed by a 100-mile hike in relentless rain. As he left Sewall to catch the train for Boston and to begin his senior year at Harvard, TR said he felt as "strong as a bull."

In his last year he took only five courses, spending as much as eight hours a day studying for them. He wrote home that he stood nineteenth in the class of 230, with "only one gentleman" ranking above him. (Apparently the other seventeen didn't count.)

He turned twenty-one that October. He had come of age, done well in everything he had tried, and had only to win Alice's consent to complete his happiness. To that end, he

★

Here, TR, a young student at Harvard, is seated beside Alice Lee, the woman he would marry. The young woman standing next to him is Rose Saltonstall, the sister of a classmate.

arranged for his family and Alice's to meet four times that fall, in New York or in Boston. They liked each other very much. Yet Alice was still standoffish; no doubt, she enjoyed keeping TR dangling. When her coming-out party after Thanksgiving drew a flock of eligible young men, TR despaired of how changeable the female mind was and spent many sleepless nights. To divert himself, he began to research and write a book he would call *The Naval War of 1812.*

On a brief trip home, TR visited with Edith Carow. After a long talk, he recorded that she was "the most cultivated, best-read girl I know." Not as slim and gay as Alice; shorter and more curvaceous. While Alice was "radiant," she was not "wise." She could not be as exciting intellectually as Edith. Were they becoming rivals in his mind?

But in January 1880 Alice agreed to marry him. "The aim of my whole life shall be to make her happy," TR recorded in his diary. Both families were delighted. TR wrote Edith the news. How she took it we do not know. She did not answer him. She had shared the growing-up years with TR, and they had been on the verge of an engagement only two years before. If terribly disappointed, she concealed her intimate feelings, as she usually did.

In June 1880 TR graduated with honors. His senior dissertation, it should be noted, was on "The Practicability of Equalizing Men and Women Before the Law." Signs of feminist leanings? Shortly before graduation he said to a friend, "I am going to try to help the cause of better government in New York City; I don't know exactly how."

The wedding was set for October 27. That summer he spent mostly with Alice. He left her in mid-August for a long-planned hunting trip out west with his brother Elliott. He had more than recreation in mind. A Cambridge physician had told TR his life was threatened by a weak heart. To live a normal span, he must quit the strenuous life and must choose an easygoing occupation.

TR was stunned. Sit around doing nothing? Become one of the idle rich? He would rather die. He would prove that the doctor was wrong.

Keeping the doctor's judgment secret, for six weeks TR and Elliott hunted wild game in Illinois, Iowa, and Minnesota. In letters home he pretended he was in fine shape, but asthma and colic assailed him. Then a snake bit him, he fell out of a wagon, and freezing rainstorms soaked him through. Still, he and Elliott managed to stuff their game bags with more than two hundred "items" each.

Returning to New York, TR switched into city dress and sped up to Boston. On October 27, 1880, he and Alice were married in a Unitarian church. The day was TR's twenty-second birthday; Alice was nineteen. They spent a quiet two weeks alone (except for the servants) at Oyster Bay. TR felt that he was "living in dreamland." He began to think of building a great house for Alice, overlooking the bay. He spent $10,000 to acquire another 60 acres there.

In November, the new couple moved into the Roosevelt home at 6 West Fifty-seventh Street, and TR began the fall term at the Columbia Law School. "I intend to be one of the governing class," he said. Yet he really had no burning desire to become a lawyer. Perhaps it was the example set by his uncle Robert, himself a lawyer. The law school at that time was way downtown. TR would walk the fifty-four blocks south to his classes each morning and then hike home in the afternoon. Sometimes he stopped at the Astor Library to do some research for his book on the naval side of the War of 1812.

Legal studies were not as demanding then as now, and TR found time to introduce Alice to New York society at dinners, parties, and balls. On snowy days they went on sleigh rides in Central Park or on Riverside Drive. Following in his father's footsteps, TR became a trustee of a hospital and an orphanage, and he joined the district club of the Republican Party, the party his father and the rest of his family favored.

When the school year ended, he and Alice went off for another honeymoon, a summer in Europe. On their return home in late September 1881, life began to change rapidly. Going into his second year at law school, TR did something unusual for a man of the upper class: he began to attend meetings of the local Republican Club. And within a month he dropped out of law school. The messy business of politics, disdained by his upper-class friends, fascinated TR. He liked the rough-and-tumble of the fight to defeat a club member, a party hack seeking renomination to the state assembly. When TR stood up to speak out against renomination, Joe Murray, one of the club leaders, spotted the young aristocrat as just the right man to convince the voters that the bad old times of machine politics were ended.

"Will you run?" asked Joe Murray.

"Wouldn't dream of it," replied TR.

But Joe Murray knew his man. A few days later, he asked again. "Yes," said TR. And because he didn't want to appear too eager, added, "But I don't want it."

Pushing the other man aside, the district party gave the nomination to TR. And on election day, he won easily. The civic groups, the "good government" people of his own class, all endorsed him. But what really helped was the Republican political machine in his district.

So here he was, an officeholder. And what was his program? Nothing, really. Only the vague belief that as an intelligent and honorable man, one who did not seek—or need—to make his living through public office, he could do good for the people.

But how? What did the people want? What did they need?

To answer that, we have to take a quick look at where TR's America stood in 1880. That year the population was 50 million, and growing very fast. Only some twenty years earlier, when TR was born and the Civil War was about to begin, the number was 30 million. The war that freed the slaves transformed the nation's industrial life. The federal government poured enormous sums into weapons, ammunition, machinery, clothing, and canned goods. To meet the urgent demand, capitalists remade old factories and built great new ones. Inventive minds devised newer, better, faster ways of manufacturing. Thousands of miles of railroads and telegraph wires knitted the country together. Industry and transporation demanded more and more iron and steel and to meet the demand, new foundries and blast furnaces transformed green fields into soot-blackened cities.

Mass-production methods were applied everywhere possible—in iron and steel, textiles and shoes, lumbering, meat packing, flour milling. Only yesterday this had been a nation of farmers, independent craftsmen, and small manufacturers living largely on the countryside. Now it was a nation of great capitalists and big factories massing wage workers in the cities.

As industry became bigger and more mechanized, skilled craftsmen saw the nature of their work change. And their wages drop. A shoemaker who once earned eighteen dollars a week now took home only twelve. In cotton mills workers got as little as five cents an hour. Women in garment shops were getting six cents for each shirt they made. And little boys working in Pennsylvania's coal mines, from dawn to dark, got one to three dollars a week.

How could people live on such wages? It cost the average working family more money to meet their expenses than they found in their pay envelopes. At the end of the week they had nothing left for clothing or entertainment, and had gone still deeper into debt. In the cities many working people lived in miserable slum conditions, their crowded rooms often used as workshops as well as homes. Near any factory, stockyard, or mine huddled the ugly tenements or shacks of the workers. Millions of slum dwellers were immigrants. The slums became "a wilderness of neglect," and as one reporter put it, "almost unexplored and almost unknown" to the people on the upper side of society.

While the number of poor had increased dramatically during this period, so had the number of rich. The richest 1 percent of the country in 1890 enjoyed wealth greater than the total of the remaining 99 percent. At the time of TR's birth, only a handful of people commanded great wealth. But thirty years later the *New York Times* counted more than four thousand millionaires.

This was how industrial capitalism was reshaping America. What did Americans think of it? The poet Walt Whitman attacked the "hollowness of heart" and the "depravity of the business classes." And Mark Twain, in his 1873 novel *The Gilded Age*, wrote that America was driven by "money lust." The moral code, he went on, was "Get rich: dishonestly if we can, honestly if we must." The men who ruled America, such critics believed, had no concern for the human beings caught in the new industrial order.

Others, however, had high praise for the success of the system. The writer W. R. Thayer claimed that the wealthy only got what they deserved. "That you have property," he wrote, "is proof of industry and foresight on your part or your father's; that you have nothing is a judgment on your laziness and vices, or on your improvidence." The poor and the unemployed, he believed, were to blame for their misery.

Well, what would TR do about this state of affairs? What *could* he—a twenty-three-year-old political novice—possibly do?

He arrived in Albany on January 2, 1882, to take his seat in the assembly. "I have become a political hack," he wrote a college friend. "But don't think I am going into politics after this year, for I am not."

4

A DUDE ENTERS POLITICS

But TR was wrong about quitting soon. "I was the youngest man there," he bragged later, "and I rose like a rocket." He found he liked the feeling of political power. As soon as he had tasted it, he wanted more, and never stopped wanting it. It didn't matter that his friends thought politics was a low-down dirty occupation. Oh, they gave money to campaigns, and they voted, but they would never rub shoulders with those rough and nasty fellows who scrambled for public office.

So it took courage for TR to choose a life his circle despised. And to stick with it long enough to master its intricacies, and to learn how to manage a political party and its members. He liked to talk about principles, but like any politician who succeeds, he found he could not always operate by them. And like many other officeholders, he always convinced himself that what he did was right, absolutely right.

TR plunged into Albany life at once. On his first appearance at a Republican caucus—a meeting of party leaders to decide on policy and candidates—he made a vivid impression. One assemblyman recorded it as follows:

> *Suddenly our eyes . . . became glued on a young man who was coming in through the door. His hair was parted in the center, and he had sideburns. He wore a single eyeglass, with a gold chain over his ear. He had on a cutaway coat with one button at the top, and the end of its tails almost reached the tops of his shoes. He carried a*

*TR, standing to the right, with other members
of the New York State Assembly*

goldheaded cane in one hand, a silk hat in the other, and he walked in the bent-over fashion that was the style with the young men of the day. His trousers were as tight as a tailor could make them, and had a bell-shaped bottom to cover his shoes.

"Who's the dude?" I asked another member, while the same question was being put in a dozen different parts of the hall.

"That's Theodore Roosevelt of New York," he answered.

There was never any doubt that TR would be a Republican. His father had been a Republican, and so had all of the family's friends. And what could the Democrats offer? In New York their political machine, run by Tammany Hall, had earned public disgrace for its open corruption. But were the Republicans any better? During the recent two terms of President Ulysses S. Grant, his Republican administration had been tarred by massive corruption. And right here in the Albany legislature TR was abruptly made aware of how corrupt state politics was. At least a third of the legislators were on the take, he figured. They made deals openly with lobbyists for the corporations. Bribes were offered and taken to pass certain bills. Legislators would even introduce bills they knew businessmen would dislike, and then take money not to pass them. The prejudices TR brought with him stand out glaringly in his observations of the assembly at work. From his diary:

The average Democrat here seems much below the average Republican. Among the professions represented in the two parties the contrast is striking. There are six liquor sellers, two bricklayers, a butcher, a tobacconist, a pawnbroker, a compositor and a typesetter in the House—all Democratic; but of the farmers and lawyers, the majority are Republicans . . . even if the worst elements of all, the twenty low Irishmen, were subtracted, the Republican average would still be higher than the Democratic.

Legislative sessions in those days were much shorter—only four months—than they are now. By the end of his first term TR felt the work was "both monotonous and stupid." His party suffered from internal quarrels, locally and nationally. TR developed a working alliance with a few other independent-minded assemblymen and with the Albany correspondent of the *New York Times.*

In March 1882, TR made the front pages of the newspapers by calling for an investigation of charges leveled against a former state attorney general and a justice of the state Supreme Court. It had to do with the way the two men had aided a scheme by the financial speculator Jay Gould, one of the notorious robber barons of that era. Gould had joined with others to gain control of the Manhattan Elevated Railway Company in a highly dubious but profitable deal.

The machine leaders of both parties were against the investigation and tried to block passage of TR's resolution. But the *Times* and other papers applied such pressure that the Judiciary Committee was forced to begin the investigation. It was only public show, for the majority voted to clear the Jay Gould crowd of any wrongdoing.

But TR's bold act of defiance made his reputation. He was no longer just that "social butterfly." The papers praised him highly, and the voters reelected him. He ran on the pledge to carry "private morality into public office."

In the assembly's next session, dominated by the Democrats, TR was chosen as Republican minority leader, making him the youngest person ever to hold that powerful position. To get things done he had to work with Grover Cleveland, the new governor, who was a Democrat. Good for both, as they held the same views on a number of issues. It was to Cleveland's advantage to have TR's support, for the governor had broken with Tammany.

A crucial issue was a bill for reform of the state's civil service system. It was badly needed to overcome what was known as the "spoils system." It was customary for political parties that won power to place their local party workers in public office as a reward for their support. The party out of power recruited people who hoped electoral success would lead to a government job. For "to the victor," it had long been said, "belong the spoils of office."

The old system meant little continuity in office. When a party organization won an election, the defeated officeholders lost their jobs, and were replaced by the winners.

After the Civil War a reform movement rose up to propose that appointments to non-policymaking positions be made from among those candidates who did best on competitive examinations, open to all. Reformers wanted hiring, advancement, and firing to be administered by a civil service commission. The reformers also asked that promotions be decided by competitive examinations.

The reform movement finally gained enough from both parties to put through Congress a federal bill, the Pendleton Civil Service Reform Act of 1883. Despite some weaknesses in the law, the new merit system transformed the federal civil service. (Later, many improvements would be enacted.)

But now reformers in New York and other states clamored for a similar law to affect state employees. Governor Cleveland supported it, while Tammany and the Republican machine combined in an effort to block it. Its only chance for success was for the reformers in both parties to unite behind it. TR rallied his independent allies to force out of committee a bill to establish a merit system. When it reached the floor, open to debate, the machine politicians were afraid to oppose it because the press and public were so strongly for it. So the bill became law.

During the Albany sessions, TR's action on labor legislation showed that his upper-class origins dominated his thinking. As he was coming of age in the 1870s, hard-fought labor battles had dominated the news. With the vast economic changes, the gap between the broad mass of working people and the new wealthy class kept widening. The old common belief in equality and independence that was part of America's revolutionary heritage was badly damaged. The growing concentration of corporate power had led to corruption in business and government. The living conditions of working people showed what a terrible human price they had paid for industrial progress.

The workers who dug the wealth out of the mines and sweated it out of the mills never shared in the benefits of the system. After the Civil War, depression after depression devastated the country and threw millions out of work. Hard times had hit first in 1867, while TR was still a boy, too young and too pampered to recognize the misery of others, and it hit again in 1873. This time the depression went so deep and so wide and lasted so long that it engulfed nearly all but the rich.

Taking advantage of mass unemployment, the nation's railroads cut wages by 35 percent and lengthened working hours while rolling up handsome dividends for their investors. Desperate, the railroad workers struck nationwide in 1877. It was the first truly national strike in American history, and the first in which the federal government massed its power—the army—on the side of business. The protest was crushed in two weeks with more than a hundred people dead. Still, the mass scale and intensity of the strike halted industry's relentless wage cutting. And the nation's business leaders learned the workers had real grievances that could not be ignored.

Business did not pick up again until 1879, when a great wave of immigrants began rolling from far-off corners of Europe into the United States. In 1880, the year TR graduated from Harvard, more than half a million immigrants landed in the promised land, and about the same large number would keep entering annually for the next decade.

Though the railroad strike created national hysteria, TR as college student seems to have ignored it, judging by his diary and letters of that period. Now, however, sitting in Albany he could not. His own city and state were centers of the growing labor movement, which pressed the legislature for bills to deal with workers' grievances.

TR was appointed to a committee to investigate tenement sweatshops in New York's cigar industry. Shocked by the terri-

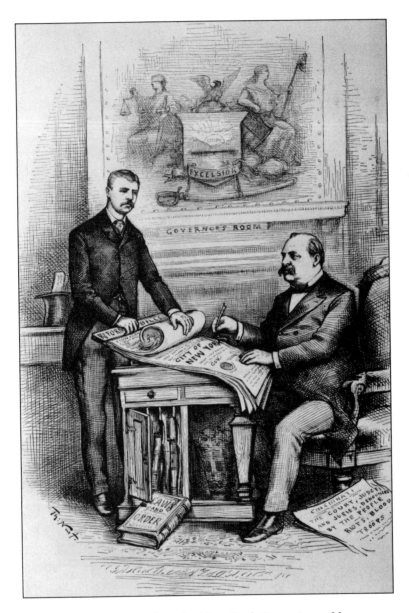

When TR served in the New York State Assembly,
he struggled to push through several reform bills and
worked closely with Governor Grover Cleveland,
who shared many of his views.

ble conditions he found on a tour of inspection, he gave support to a bill designed to abolish the making of cigars in tenement sweatshops. Later he voted for bills to limit the hours of women and children in factories and to strengthen safety measures.

But he would not venture beyond this. He even bemoaned what he called "demagogic measures . . . continually brought forward in the interests of the laboring classes." He blocked one labor bill that would have obliged the cities of New York, Brooklyn (a separate city in those days), and Buffalo to pay their employees a minimum wage of two dollars a day or twenty-five cents an hour. The expense would be too great, he said, dismissing the bill as ridiculous bunk.

TR also opposed bills to abolish labor by convicts contracted out to private employers, and to eliminate conditions close to slavery in state prisons. "Maudlin sympathy for convicts," he said. So, too, did he resist raising the pay of policemen and firemen in New York City as well as providing pensions for public school teachers. When a bill to set a twelve-hour limit on the workday of horsecar drivers in street railway systems was offered, he denounced it as a communistic idea. No red-blooded American would ask to be coddled by law, he believed.

Clearly he was no friend of the downtrodden. He was "not by nature a compassionate man," writes his biographer, Edmund Morris. "There was always something abstract about his social conscience. He 'felt' with his head rather than his heart: charity was 'a matter of practical common sense.' "

TR despised the "commercial classes," he said, because they "are only too likely to regard everything merely from the standpoint of 'Does it pay?' " But neither was he an advocate of the working people. When the labor movement united to rise up against oppression, the upheavals scared him. The historian Richard Hofstadter commented that TR's writings are dotted with tart characterizations of "extremists," "radical fanatics," "muckrakers," and "the lunatic fringe." "Sentimental humanitarians . . . always form a most pernicious body, with an influence for bad hardly surpassed by the professional criminal class."

TR was anything but stupid. Yet, thus far, he had done little thinking on social issues. He reacted almost automatically in the same way that most of his class did.

TR's young wife, Alice, had little interest in politics. In his first term at Albany he stayed at a hotel, Alice with him, but they returned to New York on most weekends. For her the city offered a great relief from the tedium of politics. In the summer of 1883, spent at Oyster Bay, she became pregnant. When TR returned to Albany for the winter session, she stayed at their newly acquired home at 55 West Forty-fifth Street. As the time for her delivery drew near, Alice moved in with her mother-in-law at Fifty-seventh Street, where TR would join her every weekend.

On Tuesday night, February 12, 1884, a girl was born. The baby was healthy, and the doctor said Alice was doing well, too. TR, in Albany, was notified and happily left for home. But by the time he arrived, close to midnight, everything had gone wrong, terribly wrong. Two of the people he loved most in the world lay dying. Alice was so sick with nephrosis, a disease affecting the kidneys, she could scarcely recognize him. In another room he found his mother in the last stage of typhoid fever, a bacterial infection. The stunned husband sat by Alice's bedside, holding her in his arms. At three o'clock that morning, TR was told his mother had died. Leaving Alice to go to his mother's bed, TR said, "There is a curse on this house." Then he went back upstairs to Alice, to continue the vigil. The next afternoon, February 14, Alice died, without recovering consciousness.

In his diary for that day, TR drew a large cross. Underneath it he wrote: "The light has gone out of my life."

Alice was twenty-two when she died, TR's mother was fifty. Two days later, after the funeral service, the two coffins were carried to Greenwood Cemetery. While others wept, TR was silent, stone-faced. He was unable to cry. He showed no interest in his baby, and could only walk up and down alone, shunning all company. The loss of Alice seemed more than he could bear. After the funeral, he wrote in his diary, "For joy or sorrow, my life has been lived out." In the next few months her name came to his lips once or twice. But by the year's end, no mention of her, ever again. Not even in his *Autobiography*, published in 1913, nearly thirty years later.

The baby, christened Alice Lee the day after the funeral, was placed in the care of TR's sister Anna. Now thirty, and unmarried, she was happy to take on the responsibility. As TR returned to Albany, Anna arranged to sell both Roosevelt houses, on Fifty-seventh and Forty-fifth streets. Soon after, TR's architect designed for him a three-story country home, with twelve bedrooms, and construction began at Oyster Bay.

In his mother's will, TR was left about half as much money as he had inherited from his father. But he would always live as though he were twice as rich. He never grasped what real money meant.

In Albany he worked at a frantic pace, fearing he would go mad from loneliness if he was not kept constantly busy. He had a hand in dozens of bills, stayed up nights to study testimony, write reports, and work on speeches. Out of the City Investigating Committee he chaired came nine reform measures to eliminate corruption in city agencies. Thanks to his leadership, all but two of these were adopted by the legislature, despite almost violent opposition.

Yet there was no happy ending. Governor Cleveland objected to the reform bills. While he thought them admirable in purpose, his careful analysis showed them to be so hastily and sloppily written that they would be ineffective as laws. When TR pushed into his office to demand that he sign the measures, the governor refused, and vetoed them instead.

Disappointed, and tired of Albany, TR declined renomination for a fourth term. He felt restless, ready to go back to private life.

But first there was his duty as delegate elected to the Republican presidential nominating convention in Chicago. There, in June of 1884, he worked closely with Henry Cabot Lodge, a Massachusetts state legislator. The two fellow aristo-

★

crats formed a close friendship that would shape political history for a long time to come. Lodge, too, was a Harvard man, a student of history, and an author. And both had giant egos and a driving ambition to rule.

In Chicago they led the independent Republicans in an effort to nominate the upright senator from Vermont, George P. Edmunds. They opposed both the incumbent, President Chester A. Arthur, and his chief rival, James Blaine of Maine. Speaker of the House of Representatives, Blaine was one of the smart operators who had built an alliance between big business and politics. Financial scandals tarnished his reputation. TR and Lodge failed to stop Blaine, who won the nomination. Furious at defeat, TR said publicly that independents like him would not give the intolerable Blaine "any support whatever." Some independents urged supporting the Democratic candidate, Grover Cleveland, while others called for a new political party, "a party of principle," to put forth a candidate.

But only a few days later, TR whistled a different tune. He told a reporter that he would support Blaine, adding that "I have been called a reformer, but I am a Republican." Although he detested Blaine, he put his party above principle. Stunned by his switch, one newspaper branded TR a "backsliding reformer" whose personal ambition had carried him to "a terrible fall."

As he always would, TR promptly called those who criticized him the victims of "moral myopia." He was the righteous one, and so were all those who now campaigned for Blaine. When a rumor spread that Cleveland had had an affair with a married woman who bore his child, Cleveland said yes, it was the truth. Whereupon TR smugly asserted that apart from politics, "for personal reasons," Cleveland was not fit to be president.

The American people disagreed. When election day came around, they chose Cleveland to be their president.

5

OUT IN THE BADLANDS

Four months after his wife's death, TR headed for the Far West. He wanted only to be alone, "far off from all mankind," riding over the prairie. A twenty-five-year-old widower, he had put his career as a politician behind him. Maybe he would begin a new life out there.

This was not his first experience in the West. He had seen it the year before, in September 1883. He had gone to the Badlands of the Dakota Territory because he had heard the region could not be matched for buffalo hunting. When he got there it was still, he said, "a land of vast silent places, of lonely rivers, and of plains where the wild game stared at the passing horsemen." But change was rapidly reshaping the country. The Indian villages had almost disappeared, to be replaced by the towns of white settlers. And the buffalo, once covering the prairie from Mexico up to Canada, no longer numbered in the millions. Now there were only a few scattered herds. Indian resistance that had blocked white settlement on the Great Plains until about 1880 had been suppressed by U.S. troops.

The region TR chose for another home was what is now southwestern North Dakota. Through it ran the Little Missouri River, fed by many creeks. Steep, jagged buttes rose up, with pines, cedars, and sagebrush climbing their sides. The layers of sandstone, clay, and marl were as multicolored as a brilliant rag rug. The weather of aeons had worn the Badlands into fantastic shapes. The prairie stretched to the horizon, a

After leaving the
New York State
Assembly, TR
headed west to the
Badlands of the
Dakota Territory,
where he vigorously
took part in buffalo
hunts and made
excursions into the
rugged interior.

vivid green in the spring, but dry and brown the rest of the almost rainless year. Summers were terribly hot, and winters terribly cold. The temperature could soar up to 125 degrees or plummet down to 40 degrees below zero.

To go on a buffalo hunt was TR's long-held dream. Although the weather was foul when he arrived, he and his guide rode day after day through heavy rains without catching sight of a single buffalo. Despite cold, hunger, thirst, and fatigue, TR never complained. "This is fun!" he said to his guide. He fell in love with the Badlands. Only at the end of the second week of hunting did he spy a big buffalo and shoot it. This first success made him almost hysterically happy. He removed the skin and head for shipment to a New York taxidermist.

When he arrived in Little Missouri—a four-eyed eastern dude—he was greeted coldly. But by the time he left, his good humor and endurance had won over the tough westerners. He felt like a man among men in this wild country. "Here," he said later, "the romance of my life began."

But not only romance; he decided he could make money in the business of cattle ranching. He put up the funds to buy cattle. Yet there was another side to this experience, however brief. It may have set him to thinking about conservation. He had seen how scarce the buffalo and other large animals were in the Dakota Territory. And he knew their disappearance had been caused by uncontrolled slaughter. Couldn't something be done to protect and preserve the natural world? With his return to Dakota after Alice's death, his black mood began to lift. He would spend a dozen hours a day in the saddle, looking after his cattle business. He felt the chance of making it a success was very good. To his sister Anna, who was taking care of little Alice back home, he wrote:

> *The country is growing on me, more and more; it has a curious, fantastic beauty of its own, and as I own six or eight horses I have a fresh one every day and ride on a lope all day long. How sound I sleep at night now! There is not much game, however; the cattle men have crowded it out and only a few antelope and deer remain. I have shot a*

few jackrabbits and curlews, with the rifle, and I also killed eight rattlesnakes.

He expanded his stock, investing so much money—almost half his inheritance—that the family back home began to worry. He added another fifteen hundred cattle and bought some land on which to build his Elkhorn Ranch house. From now through 1892, he would divide his time between New York and Dakota. For the first several years he spent more time in the West, savoring it in all seasons, than in the East.

He tried to transform himself into his ideal image of the true frontiersman, hiring a tailor to make him a buckskin suit. For years he wore it on hunting trips, telling everyone how sturdy, comfortable, and traditional it was: "It was the dress in which Daniel Boone was clad when he first passed through the trackless forests of the Alleghenies and penetrated into the heart of Kentucky; it was the dress worn by grim old Davy Crockett when he fell at the Alamo."

TR's Elkhorn Ranch in the Dakota Territory,
as depicted by artist Frederic Remington

During those years TR made six trips into the mountains to the west of Dakota. The first was to the Big Horn Mountains of Wyoming; then to the Coeur d'Alenes of Idaho; the Selkirks of British Columbia; the Bitterroots of Wyoming and Idaho; Yellowstone National Park, created by Congress in 1872; and, finally, to the Two-Ocean Pass country of Wyoming.

Such trips required long preparation, lots of equipment, and the help of teamsters and guides. TR's aim was to obtain trophies—the heads of the larger game animals with which wealthy men like himself loved to decorate their homes and offices.

Day after day he filled his diary with the record of animals, big and small, that he had shot. Duck, grouse, teal, whitetail and blacktail bucks, does, jackrabbits, elk—in less than fifty bloodthirsty days he ran up a total of 170 animals. But what he wanted to kill most of all was the Rocky Mountain grizzly bear, the most dangerous animal in North America. One fall day, while out on the trail, he almost collided head-on with a 9-foot, 1,200-pound grizzly. He tells what happened:

> *Doubtless my face was pretty white, but the blue barrel was as steady as a rock as I glanced along it until I could see the top of the head fairly between his two sinister-looking eyes; as I pulled the trigger I jumped aside out of the smoke, to be ready if he charged; but it was needless, for the great brute was struggling in the death agony. . . . The bullet hole in his skull was exactly between his eyes as if I had measured the distance with a carpenter's rule.*

But TR's interests went beyond hunting. He studied the features of strange landscapes and made careful notes on plant and animal life. The true hunter, he said, "should be a lover of nature as well as of sport, or he will miss half the pleasure of being in the woods."

He could tune in to wildlife with the intensity of a Thoreau. Here he describes almost lyrically what he felt when he first heard the bugling of an elk:

It is a most singular and beautiful sound, and is very much the most musical cry uttered by any four-footed beast. When heard for the first time it is almost impossible to believe that it is the call of an animal; it seems far more as if by an Aeolian harp or some strange wind instrument. It consists of a series of notes uttered continuously, in a most soft, musical, vibrant tone, so clearly that they can be heard half a mile off. Heard in the clear, frosty moonlight from the depths of the rugged and forest-clad mountains the effect is most beautiful, for its charm is heightened by the wild and desolate surroundings. It has the sustained, varied melody of some bird songs, with, of course, a hundred-fold greater power.

Most of the trophies that TR hunted he managed to get: the heads of the Big Horn, the Rocky Mountain goat, caribou, grizzly bear. He took on community responsibility, too, helping to organize a group of ranchers to introduce law and order and to put down cattle thieves. Appointed a deputy sheriff in 1885, he captured three thieves who had stolen one of his boats. After chasing them for "three days of acute misery" in wintry weather, he caught up with them. On hand was a camera to record the chase and the triumphant young rancher standing guard with his gun over the culprits. It was a boy's dream that he was living.

Each year, by the time autumn came on, the sun burned the prairie grass dry and brittle. Fires broke out easily. In the fall of 1885 the ranchers in TR's area counted many more than usual, especially on a long stretch of grassland over which the cowboys drove the herds to the railheads. The stock lost much weight, since they couldn't graze on the blackened prairie. It caused a sharp drop in profits. The ranchers were convinced that Indians had set the fires to protest the whites' invasion of their ancient hunting grounds.

TR reacted in the same way as the other ranchers. He didn't understand the Native Americans, their culture, their tradition, their necessities. Nor did he respect their rights:

During the past century a good deal of sentimental nonsense has been talked about our taking the Indians' land. Now, I do not mean to say for a moment that gross wrong has not been done the Indians, both by government and individuals, again and again. . . . Where brutal and reckless frontiersmen are brought into contact with a set of treacherous, vengeful and fiendishly cruel savages a long series of outrages on both sides is sure to follow. But as regards the taking of the land, at least from the Western Indians, the simple truth is that the latter never had any real ownership in it at all. . . . The Indians should be treated in just such a way that we treat the white settlers. Give each his little claim; if, as would generally happen, he declined this, why, then let him share the lot of the thousands of white hunters and trappers who have lived on the game that the settlement of the country has exterminated, and let him like these whites, perish from the face of the earth which he cumbers.

In the winter of 1886–1887 the worst weather that old-timers could recall struck the Little Missouri region. It killed off cattle by the tens of thousands. Some of the cowhands, searching for cattle in the blizzards, never got back home. A few people, penned up in their cabins by the unrelenting storms, went insane. TR was not there to see the disaster. When he reached Elkhorn Ranch in April 1887, as the snows were melting, he found his losses were terrible, costing him at least $50,000. That ended his experiment in ranching.

But it was an experiment that brought other rewards. Life in the West had changed TR. His way of fighting against his doctor's grim prediction had won out. He was no longer the dude in elegant clothes who talked in the affected drawl of a New York aristocrat. He was a rugged, husky, broad-shouldered man who looked and acted like the man who could ride the range for weeks and match the toughest cowboys in skill and endurance.

Deputy Sheriff Roosevelt just after he had taken, "absolutely by surprise," the three lawbreakers who had stolen his boat. Ever mindful of publicity, he had brought along his camera to record the adventure.

On his earlier visits home he had almost ignored his little daughter, Alice. None of his letters from Dakota asked about her. Perhaps because, as everyone noted, little Alice looked so much like her mother, he was afraid to be reminded of what he had lost.

By the time he gave up ranching, his house at Oyster Bay was completed. It would be his permanent home for the rest of his life. The house sat on a hilltop, with the summer houses of relatives visible through the trees. He called the home Sagamore Hill after an Indian chief of long ago whose territory this had been. TR's friends noted a new happiness in him, as though something vital that had almost been extinguished had been ignited again. And it had, for he was in love.

6

"WRITING IS HORRIBLY HARD WORK"

It was in the early fall of 1885 that TR and Edith Carow met again, by chance. For nineteen months they had not seen each other. Between them lay an old romance that had ended abruptly, and the death of his beloved Alice Lee. What their feelings were at this encounter one can only guess. But soon TR began calling on her, and before long he proposed, and she accepted. "I have never loved anyone else," she wrote to him. "I love you with the passion of a girl who has never loved before." Still, they decided to keep their engagement a secret from everyone and to postpone marriage for a time. Widowed for less than two years, TR felt it would not look right for him to remarry so soon. So while he returned to his Dakota ranch, she went abroad with her mother and sister.

What made their separation easier was the chance to do some work of the kind he loved. A publisher asked him to write a life of Thomas Hart Benton, a Missouri statesman of Andrew Jackson's time who stood for expansion in the West. While meeting all the demands of a ranchman's business, TR kept working on the book. "Writing is horribly hard work to me," he told a friend. But he finished the 85,000-word biography by July of 1886.

Published the next year, it was TR's third book. Its research is faulty by today's scholarly standards. But reading it now, you can see how closely he identified with those traits of Benton the frontiersman that were so like his own—"in-

Edith Carow at the time of her marriage to TR

tense pride in country . . . masterful spirit . . . American to his heart's core." Like Benton, TR believed in manifest destiny, the "right" of the American republic to expand to all the lands hemming in our territory. He regretted that we did not gobble up Canada, for "we were the people who could use it best, and we ought to have taken it all."

TR's writing is a side of the man most people today are scarcely aware of. He made himself as much a professional author as a professional politician. He published thirty-eight books— history, natural science, biography, political philosophy, essays on anything and everything. His first book, *The Naval War of 1812*, begun when he was only twenty-one, is considered a classic. The conclusions he drew from that research reshaped, in later years, the U.S. Navy. His multivolume study, *The Winning of the West*, was also based on sound research and is still highly rated. Begun in January 1888, it covers the first two centuries of American history and took him seven years to write.

Although TR called for writers to use an objective pen, he himself often let his political prejudices distort his work. He looked for precedents to justify what he wished to do as a politician, and attacked those whose views differed from his own. In his writing and reading, as in his life, he measured others by his personal code of behavior. He made no allowance for figures of the past whose spirit and even vocabulary expressed a different society's viewpoint. He believed a true American's work should be strenuous, manly, patriotic. He called the English poet Chaucer "needlessly filthy," said the Revolution's pamphleteer Tom Paine was "a filthy little atheist," and novelist Henry James was "a very despicable creature."

Of the years TR spent in the West he left a personal account that fills three volumes. They play up his adventures while hunting, but do much more. For they contain the stories of birds and small mammals and big game whose life patterns he continued to observe with the same concentration and skill shown in childhood.

Some of TR's books are considered superficial and hasty. Few people read them any longer. They are faulted for occasional bad grammar and overuse of superlatives. At times he accepted as fact the statements of others he should have checked for accuracy. He was conscious of his weaknesses as a writer. "Although I have on the whole done fairly well at it," he wrote to a friend, "I should like to write some book that would really rank in the very first class, but I suppose this is a mere dream."

While writing occupied much of TR's time now, he still relished the excitement of political action. He plunged back into the game in the fall of 1886 when a group of influential Republicans induced him to run for mayor of New York. This request took him by surprise. What about Edith and the three-month honeymoon in Europe they had planned? But always a loyal Republican, he could not say no.

TR's backers were of course opposed to the Tammany machine candidate, Abram Hewitt, a wealthy manufacturer. But this time they worried much more about a third-party candidate named Henry George, the best-known radical in America.

Henry George had published *Progress and Poverty* in 1879, one of the most widely read books in American history. It sold millions of copies around the world. In his book George singled out private ownership of land as the main cause of inequality and corruption. He said that any increase in land values was due merely to the growth of the community, and that so-called unearned increment should be taken by the government for the benefit of all. All other taxes would be abolished—hence, the "single tax." But it wasn't simply this proposal that made him so popular. It was his steady drumming on the central problems that the great majority of Americans faced—poverty and inequality.

George's mayoral campaign excited tremendous enthusiasm among the city's working people, especially the trade unionists. They were impatient with liberals who would not approve governmental action in behalf of the poor. Now, for the first time, they had a Labor Party candidate, a candidate of their own. The election came in a year when hundreds of thousands of working people had gone out on some 1,500 strikes nationwide, demanding an eight-hour working day.

That spring at a mass rally in Chicago's Haymarket Square, protesting police brutality against strikers at a local factory, a bomb had exploded, killing seven policemen and wounding many others. Eight radical and anarchist workers were indicted for the bombing, though no proof was ever offered of their responsibility. Out on his ranch at the time, TR wrote a friend that his cowboys were "true Americans through and through. I believe nothing would give them greater pleasure than a chance with rifles at one of the mobs." Later he said it would be best for all Americans "that the Chicago dynamiters be hung."

At the same time, the labor movement had mounted a series of boycotts to win concessions from employers by persuading other workers to stop patronizing their business. The New York courts ruled boycotting a form of criminal conspiracy and banned it. Stiff prison sentences were given workers for violating the law. Workers had no voice in decisions that affected their lives. And now if they dared protest, they were crushed by business leaders in alliance with government.

The mayoral campaign lasted only one month. George spoke to labor and church groups more than one hundred times, often appearing at five meetings in one night. Trying to channel working-class protest into political action, he said:

All men who work for a living, whether by hand or head, are underpaid. Labor nowhere has its full and fair reward. Everywhere the struggle for existence, the difficulty of making a living, is far greater than it ought to be. This cannot be remedied by my election for Mayor; but a start will have been made; we shall at least have begun. From that time forth the questions of work and wages, the questions that concern the earnings and the livings of us all, will get such attention as they never had before. And the men who work for a living will have become conscious of the power of these questions.

The hope that George offered working people was that only by the ballot could they obtain "the redress of their political and social grievances."

After surveying his chances, TR concluded it was "a perfectly hopeless contest." Still, he was a fighter, and maybe if he gave it all he had, by some miracle he might win. Besides, it would not be so bad if he came in second. After all, he couldn't possibly come in third. That would be a true disaster.

So he campaigned as hard as he could, putting in eighteen-hour days, speaking at rally after rally in a single evening, holding press conferences, planning strategy, writing letters, checking on leaflet copy. Responding to Henry George's speeches, he denied there was a class issue and that employers ruthlessly exploited workers. If labor wanted to solve its problems, then it must rely on more of "that capacity for steady, industrious self-help which is the glory of every true American." He had yet to admit that the poor and the unemployed were not to blame for their condition and that there were social causes for the troubles afflicting masses of Americans.

By contrast, Henry George said, "The true purpose of government is, among other things, to give everyone security that he shall enjoy the fruits of his labor, to prevent the strong from oppressing the weak, and the unscrupulous from robbing the honest. . . . What we are beginning here is the great American struggle for the ending of industrial slavery."

When an independent survey of the way voters were leaning came out, it showed that Henry George was making a remarkably good race. The Republican bigwigs were alarmed. The last thing they wanted to see was a labor man, a radical at that, in the mayor's seat. The party bosses quietly put out the word: Republicans, vote for Hewitt! TR soon heard that he was being sold out by his own party. But he kept silent.

When the final returns came in, Hewitt had won with 91,000 votes, George was second with 68,000, and TR last, with 60,000. The turnout was immense, yet TR's vote was lower than that for any other Republican candidate in the past six years. Even his own district had thrown votes to the Democrat. One historian suggests that very possibly George got a majority of the legal votes, but was counted out by Tammany Hall.

TR barely mentions that election in his *Autobiography*. It was too painful to recall.

A few days later, he boarded a Cunard liner for England. On December 2, 1886, he and Edith were married at Saint George's Church in London. Very few guests attended the quiet wedding.

7

FAMILY LIFE IN WASHINGTON

The honeymoon—TR's second—lasted four months. The couple spent much of it in England, where high society welcomed them. They wintered on the Riviera and then toured Italy.

It was while they were abroad that TR learned of the terrible blizzard that had ruined his ranching business and wiped out his heavy investment. What should he do? Sell Sagamore Hill? Cut down on all his expenses? Earn money somehow? Edith did not panic; she had learned how to make do with very little when her alcoholic father had died and left his family with next to nothing. She figured they could keep Sagamore Hill by managing their lives a lot less expensively.

They came home in March 1887, with Edith pregnant. Her first baby, a boy, was born that September and named Theodore Roosevelt, Jr. Into their home came little Alice, too. When Edith learned TR had offered to give Alice permanently into his sister's care, she was very upset. She insisted that Alice must come live with them. "It almost broke my heart to give her up," said TR's sister.

In the next ten years Edith would have four more children—Kermit, Ethel, Archibald, and Quentin. TR was the center of their world. Naturally playful (hadn't a friend said he was still a seven-year-old in a man's body?), he improvised all sorts of games with his children, told them stories of his boyhood heroes and his adventures out west, read books to

*Soon after the death of Alice Lee, TR had a
house constructed for himself in Oyster Bay, New
York. It was completed by the time he returned from
the Dakota Territory, and he named it Sagamore Hill,
after an Indian chief who had once lived on this land.*

them, took them on long nature walks and overnight outings, introduced them to riding and boating and tennis.

Edith's temperament was different. She took on all the worries about meeting bills as the family kept growing. While TR was happiest in company, especially that of men, she was more of a loner. They had to find ways to reconcile their differences. "Most of the time she was kind and considerate," wrote one biographer, "but she could also be demanding and possessive. Some family friends thought her ruthless in the way she took over her husband's life, pushing his adoring sisters out of it."

Edith suffered from migraine headaches, and when they ravaged her, she could be hard on both husband and children. Nevertheless, their marriage was a happy one. More than thirty years after their engagement, TR said, "I really think I am just as much in love with her as I was then—she is so nice and good and pretty and charming." (Not a tribute a modern feminist would appreciate.)

That year, when he was establishing a family, was a restless time for TR. He worked hard to complete the first volume of *The Winning of the West*. But he longed to get back into politics. He volunteered to campaign in the Midwest for Benjamin Harrison, the Republican candidate for president. The Democrats' nominee was Grover Cleveland, who proposed reducing the high tariffs that protected America's corporations from foreign competition. While TR made speeches, Republican party leaders raised huge sums from big business to ensure their man's election. Much of the money went into key states to buy votes and to stuff ballot boxes. It worked: although Cleveland got the majority of the popular vote, Harrison narrowly won enough electoral votes to put him in the White House.

TR hoped that what he did for his party would earn him a political job. When powerful friends put in a good word for him, Harrison appointed him one of the three U.S. Civil Service commissioners. The job paid only $3,500 a year, but even that amount was badly needed by the Roosevelts. TR eagerly accepted. In May 1889 he left the family at Oyster Bay and reported for duty in Washington.

He would hold that job for six long years. Out to make his commission "a living force," TR said he would enforce the law "up to the handle, everywhere, fearlessly and honestly." In trying to do that, he showed a great gift for public relations, using every means possible to advance his cause in the media.

Although only thirty, with the other two commissioners much his senior in age and in service, TR quickly became the dominant force, stirring up turmoil, fussing and feuding with everyone who differed with him, and grabbing the headlines.

The commission's job was to administer the Pendleton Act of 1883. TR soon saw that, despite the law, politics and patronage still controlled a great many federal jobs. Whichever party came to power packed the bureaucracy with its faithful followers. Even before TR could warm his seat, John Wanamaker, the party's chief fund-raiser and now the postmaster general, had kicked out thirty thousand fourth-class postmasters and replaced them with deserving Republicans.

TR got into a long feud with Wanamaker almost at once. Investigation unearthed corruption among twenty-five postal officials in Baltimore. TR demanded they be fired, while Wanamaker tried to shield them. The president did not want to anger such a big fund-raiser, so he said nothing and did nothing. Two years later a congressional committee upheld TR, and the press and the reformers applauded him. No thanks to President Harrison, whom TR dismissed as "a genial little runt."

When Edith brought the family down to Washington, they moved into a small house, all they could afford. Now TR was too burdened with his office to continue writing, and they missed even the modest income his books and articles had brought in. Edith continued to have babies, which upset some of their closest friends. They thought it "reckless" and "a shame" to have so many children "without the means either to educate or provide for them."

Edith placed her husband on a daily allowance, but he never knew where his money went. She scrimped on everything, even making their own tooth powder. Paying for the upkeep of both Sagamore Hill and the Washington house and moving his family back and forth twice a year brought them close to bankruptcy. TR began to think he should never have gone into politics. It was really a career only for the rich.

As if his financial worries were not enough, the troubles of his brother Elliott, long a family concern, became intolerable. He was a chronic drunk, sliding from one crisis into another. Urged to take the cure for alcoholism in a sanitarium,

★

Elliott refused and went off to Europe with his wife and two children. His wife, pregnant again, feared that he would harm her in one of his drunken rages. Although Elliott was in and out of asylums abroad and then at home, his life plunged downhill with terrifying speed. His wife died of diphtheria in 1892, a son died of the same disease a year later, and finally a convulsive attack killed Elliott himself. Left almost alone in the world was their daughter Eleanor, later to marry her cousin, Franklin Delano Roosevelt.

The series of disasters shook up TR badly. He had felt bitter toward his brother for a long time, but now he grieved for the loss of the childhood sweetness between them.

Washington was then a southern city of some 200,000 people. At least 60,000 were African-Americans, who lived mostly in the alleys behind the patrician squares. (Today the capital numbers 600,000 residents). Wealthy or not, the Roosevelts could count on social prestige to open doors to them. TR's unique personality made him popular with the rich and powerful. He and Edith dined out often, enjoyed suppers and balls and theater parties, mixing with the top officials of government and the ambassadors of foreign powers. They could afford to give only small dinner parties, served without champagne, but who cared? Their guest lists included "the best people," meaning those with power, breeding, and brains.

Among their special friends were Senator Lodge, of course; Henry Adams, historian and grandson and great-grandson of presidents; John Hay, Lincoln's secretary and biographer; Tom Reed, Speaker of the House; the sculptor Augustus Saint-Gaudens; and the painter John La Farge. TR was always welcome in their homes, for, as one of them said, "There was a vital radiance about the man, a glowing unfeigned cordiality toward those he liked that was irresistible."

TR not only did his best to uproot corruption but tried to improve the merit system itself. He revised the examinations that people took to win a place on the eligible lists. He believed they should focus more on practical necessities than on theoretical issues. Skill in spelling and arithmetic wouldn't be of much use to a border patrolman if he couldn't ride a horse or shoot a gun.

As the merit system expanded, it freed the political parties from financial dependence on their appointees, who usually gave a portion of their pay back to the party. But without these kickbacks, the parties became increasingly dependent for support upon financial contributions from big business. (And that's more true than ever today, more than a hundred years later.)

When the presidential election of 1892 came on, Grover Cleveland was again nominated by the Democrats. The Republicans renominated President Harrison, though with little enthusiasm. Ever loyal, TR campaigned for Harrison, viciously attacking Cleveland in his speeches. When Cleveland won in November, TR feared the new president would not renew his appointment as civil service commissioner. Surprisingly, he did. Why? Because he sincerely believed in the merit system, and TR had fought for it. Still, what more could TR do? The work was getting to be a bore; six years was long enough.

He began to look for another job.

★

8

NEW YORK'S TOP COP

What could be more exciting for TR than to become top cop of his hometown? True, he was appointed just one of New York's four police commissioners. But when was he ever content to play second fiddle? The public saw TR as the man who could clean up the police department and make New York a safe and decent place in which to live and work.

He took office in May 1895. His appointment can be traced back to two happenings. One was his personal experience serving in the state legislature, during which time he had headed an investigation of the city's police force. Witness after witness reported how badly the police department was run and how corrupt the force was. After hearing that testimony, TR was convinced the city needed police reform.

Then, in 1892, the Reverend Charles H. Parkhurst launched from the pulpit an attack upon the city as "a very hotbed of knavery, debauchery and bestiality." The police scandals he described so vividly inspired another investigation that revealed even more corruption than TR had unearthed. This investigation led to the formation of a fusion ticket meant to unseat the Tammany machine running City Hall. The reform mayoral candidate, William L. Strong, a businessman, won in 1894. Tammany was defeated—temporarily.

This was a time when the big cities were notorious centers of political corruption and crime. If you went to almost any city, from New York to San Francisco, you'd hear the same sad story. City councils for sale. Municipal services, such as water, gas, and street railways, granted for long terms to private corporations with the authority to charge exorbitant rates. Mayors protecting criminals. Police whose salaries were only a fraction of their income due to graft. And politicians who knew how to get the votes needed to keep the system going.

The victims of the graft and corruption were all but the rich. The people saw their taxes soar, their water contaminated, their sewage systems fouled, their streetcars scheduled haphazardly, their city made ugly with badly paved streets and jerry-built tenements.

But was it true that political corruption fouled only the cities? Many people believed this. They thought the cities were a threat to democracy and good government. TR reported from his experience in the New York legislature that the worst of his colleagues came from the big cities and were "very low indeed . . . usually foreigners of little or no education, with exceedingly misty ideas as to morality." TR's notion of rural purity and urban corruption was shaped by the racist thinking of his time. The early arrivals in America, those of Nordic or Aryan stock from western Europe, like TR's family, were born to be leaders, he believed. The later arrivals from eastern and southern Europe now flooding in were of inferior stock, he thought, dependent on political bosses because they were peasants untrained for urban life.

This tidal wave of new immigration was not only a huge addition to the American population in numbers but a spectacular shift in source. The newcomers rarely spoke English, and most were Catholic or Jewish. Few meant to settle on the land. Most would find work as unskilled or semiskilled laborers in the urban centers. In just a single decade, 1880–1890, the urban population soared from 14 million to 22 million nationwide. By 1900, one out of every three Americans would be a city dweller.

Many who entered the port of New York City simply stayed there. The city rapidly increased. Like other cities, it

*Toward the end of the nineteenth century,
a great wave of immigrants from eastern and
southern Europe arrived in the United States.*

grew so incredibly fast that local government could not keep up with the enormous pressure for the new services needed. Bidders for municipal contracts offered big money for monopoly control.

It wasn't the immigrants who caused the corruption. No, it was closely bound up with the growing influence of big business at the municipal level as well as at the state and national levels. As Lincoln Steffens, an investigative reporter of that time, wrote about one political boss:

> *His business was boodling, which is a more refined and*
> *a more dangerous form of corruption than police blackmail.*
> *It involves, not thieves, gamblers and common women, but*
> *influential citizens, capitalists, and great corporations. For*
> *the stock-in-trade of the boodler is the rights, privileges,*
> *franchises, and real property of the city, and his source of*
> *corruption is the top, not the bottom, of society.*

Nor was it true that corruption was confined to the big cities. The rural state of New Hampshire, to give but one instance, was notoriously boss-ruled. The purchase of rural votes was common. So common, said Rhode Island's governor, that nobody tried to conceal it. The people who sold their votes saw it as a form of social security, as this doggerel suggests:

> *Many people sold their vote*
> *For to buy an overcoat,*
> *Or to buy a sack of flour,*
> *Thinking it a prosperous hour.*

So political corruption had its social roots. But TR, writing in a magazine, held that neither "capital" nor "labor" but the individual was responsible for dishonest government. Bent on rooting up corruption, Mayor Strong wanted TR to head the Police Board, and at its first meeting he was made its president. Reform would replace the spoils system. The young TR— thirty-six now—independent and courageous, would clean out the civic sewers that corrupted the system.

Police headquarters was on Mulberry Street then, in the heart of the worst slums. It was as gloomy as a medieval dungeon and the holding cells below ground were a playground for rats and vermin. The cops on the beat, barely able to read and write, got their jobs through the Tammany machine. They were on the take, getting payoffs from saloonkeepers, gamblers, pimps, and prostitutes.

TR could expect stiff resistance from a department threatened by honest administration. From the first day on the job,

*A cartoonist depicts Police Commissioner Roosevelt
on guard at the headquarters on Mulberry Street.*

he was all action. One of his moves was to do something about
the homeless people. Thousands lived on the streets, having
been tossed out of their jobs by the long depression that had
begun in 1893. At night the police stations opened their
basements to men who had no other place to sleep. Jacob Riis,
a crusading reporter who became close to TR, had long battled
for closing the police shelters. One morning at two o'clock,
he took TR on a visit to a police lodging room. On the bare
stone floor of the filthy basement TR saw men lying side by
side. Riis told him such conditions were the seedbed of disease.
At times typhus broke out in the basements and then was

spread in the morning from door to door as the jobless begged for their breakfast. Though health officials and the charitable societies denounced the evils of the basement shelters, the city said it had no money to build lodging houses for the homeless poor.

Appalled by what he saw, TR said to Riis that night, "I will smash them tomorrow!" The next morning he ordered the police stations to shut down the basement shelters. (But no provision was made for the homeless to be housed elsewhere.)

TR's midnight wanderings in the streets gave him great pleasure. After dining out, he would rise from his host's table, toss a black cloak over his evening clothes, pull a broad-brimmed hat low over his eyes, and sail out of the room to stalk the streets on a personal inspection tour. He often found patrolmen asleep, away from their beat, or chatting comfortably with a prostitute. His disguise deceived many a policeman who made the mistake of getting belligerent when this stranger questioned him. Imagine the effect upon the unwary cop when TR revealed who he was. The next day the victim would have to appear before TR for judgment.

Such colorful exploits pleased the citizens who read about them day after day. How often had they wished for the power to put down an arrogant police officer! TR's fame as the bold and virtuous knight spread across the country. He'd make a fine senator, people said. Or maybe even president.

Touring the slums in Riis's company, TR saw enough to make him join in condemnation of the rickety and rat-ridden tenements. He began to read reports on other social conditions as well. The labor troubles that arose out of the depression of the nineties tormented him. He was angered by the callousness of those in his class who flaunted their wealth shamelessly. When the Bradley Martins gave a grand ball at the Waldorf-Astoria in 1897 the host wore a suit of gold brocade while one of his guests paraded around the room in a suit of gold inlaid armor valued at $10,000. This in the midst of the black cloud of hunger and unemployment that hung over the city. TR called such display a needless provocation to the poor.

★

Jacob Riis, a news reporter who had emigrated
from Denmark, investigated the miserable living
conditions of America's new arrivals.

But when the working poor refused to take low wages passively and went on strike, TR was just as angry. He hated disorder of any kind. He clashed with labor time and again over the way he policed strikes. Once, he told a reporter: "We shall guard as zealously the rights of the striker as those of the employer. But when riot is menaced, it is different. The mob takes its own chance. Order will be kept at whatever cost. If it comes to shooting, we shall shoot to hit. No blank cartridges or firing over the head of anybody."

TR ran into trouble when he announced he would enforce the Sunday law meant to stop the sale of liquor on the Sabbath. His desire to enforce every law, whether good or bad, had nothing to do with ending drinking itself. He didn't believe a law could control that. But what started him on his campaign was the common knowledge that the Sunday law was a source of corruption. The police took bribes from the saloonkeepers to let them do business on the Sabbath. Those pub owners who refused to buy protection were raided.

The saloon was the place where working people met. (The upper classes drank at home, in private clubs, or in expensive hotels.) It was where workers, mostly male, came together to drink, to see their friends, to read a paper, to pick up a lead for a job. The saloons promoted alcoholism, of course, and diverted wages from the family to support the drinking. But they were a vital part of working-class culture. Many politicians set up their unofficial headquarters in them, handing out favors in the back rooms and buying "the boys" a drink at the bar.

By arresting saloonkeepers, TR trashed his popularity. Working people wanted to know why the upper classes could get anything they wanted at their private clubs while the less fortunate had to go dry in these hot summer months. To make TR look ridiculous, his political enemies invoked through the courts those long-neglected Sunday laws that required soda fountains, florists, and delicatessens to stay closed on the Sabbath. Silly as those blue laws were, now TR had to order his police to chase the violators.

By December 1895, TR was lamenting the fact that "not one New York City newspaper or one New York City politician is on my side." Mayor Strong urged him to let up on the saloons, implying he would fire him if he didn't. His position became even shakier when his quarrels with the other police commissioners became a public nuisance.

In mid-1896, TR wrote his sister that "the work of the Police Board . . . is as grimy as all work for municipal reform over here must be for some decades to come; it is inconceivably arduous, disheartening and irritating." He lacked the "absolute power" he craved to do any job.

He felt he had been out of touch with "the life of the great world and with national politics." Yes, he had done some good locally in these years, but now he longed for a role on a bigger stage.

How would he get it? Who would give it to him?

9

A GREAT CAMPAIGNER

If his brief years as police commissioner fizzled out, they did have some good effect upon TR. Through the eyes of Jacob Riis, he had seen on the Lower East Side an America he had known nothing about. No longer could this aristocrat believe that social problems were not the concern of government. Now, he said, he distrusted "those men, whether business men, or lawyers, judges, legislators or executive officers who seek to make the constitution a fetish for the prevention of the work of social reform."

Although his own party leaders had come to dislike him, his dramatic exploits on Mulberry Street had made him a national figure. As his biographer Henry Pringle said, "He had earned a just reputation for vigor and for honesty, if not for good sense or diplomacy, and this was of value when the lightning struck."

The lightning would strike soon. The stormy times building up to it reached a climax in 1896. It was a decisive political year. The battle line over which way the country should go was drawn sharply between the Republican and Democratic parties.

Signs of the coming struggle for power became clear to many Americans when they read Henry George's passionate portrait of hard times. Then, in 1887, came Edward Bellamy's *Looking Backward,* a utopian novel set in the year 2000. It showed what life could be like if the social, political, and economic systems were organized to eliminate poverty, disease, and corruption. Countless Americans read it and absorbed its lessons.

In 1892 a new party, the Populist or People's Party, was born with a program for making America over. Its slogan was "We Do Not Ask For Sympathy or Pity: We Ask for Justice." Joined mostly by farmers in the West and South whose life had been made miserable by the railroads, the mortgage companies, the trusts, and the middlemen, it got nearly a million votes that year. Although the Democrat Grover Cleveland was elected president, the Populists elected governors in four western states, sent two senators and eleven congressmen to Washington, and seated hundreds of Populists in nineteen state legislatures.

With the 1893 depression, Populist support increased. It worried the Democrats looking to the 1894 election; they began to endorse certain parts of the Populist platform in order to win back old followers. Still, the Republicans managed to get the support of urban workers by appealing directly to their narrow economic interests and their ethnic loyalties. They promised renewed prosperity and jobs for all.

It worked. Although the Populist vote in 1894 rose to 1.5 million, the Republicans won the biggest victory in the history of Congress. The Democrats were overwhelmed. The old two-party deadlock that had dominated American politics since the end of the Civil War was ended. The Republicans now held majority power.

To the "respectable people" who voted Republican, the rise of Populism was frightening. They hadn't forgotten the Haymarket bombing of 1886. Nor had they forgotten July 1892, when a battle between three hundred armed Pinkerton guards and the workers at the Carnegie Homestead Steel mill had resulted in ten men killed and seventy wounded. And two weeks later the anarchist Alexander Berkman had severely wounded the Carnegie superintendent Henry Clay Frick in an assassination attempt. On top of all this had come the panic of 1893 and the breadlines, and then the Pullman strike of 1894 in which President Cleveland had used federal troops to

The *1892* strike at the Carnegie Homestead Steel mill turned
bloody when a clash between hundreds of workers and armed
Pinkerton guards left ten dead and more than seventy wounded.

*When the Pullman Palace Car Company cut wages
by 25 percent, the American Railway Union went
on strike, but when workers in Chicago threatened
to prevent mail trains from passing, President Grover
Cleveland called on federal troops to guard them.*

move the mails and smash the strike. And hadn't General Jacob Coxey of Ohio led his "Coxey's Army" of the unemployed in a march on Washington to demand federal relief?

Was revolution around the corner? Nonsense, said Mark Hanna, the big boss of the Republican Party. TR agreed. All these rebels against the system were "strikingly like the leaders of the French Revolution in mental and moral attitude," he said, but they didn't have the power to carry out their ideas.

As the election campaign of 1896 drew near, TR hoped that if a Republican won the presidency, he might be given some high-level job. Surely not a cabinet post, for he had become too politically unpopular in New York for that. But what about assistant secretary of the navy? He believed American security was endangered by developments in the Caribbean and the Atlantic. If he could get the navy post, he was sure he could do something about that threat.

The mood of America was tense as the election campaign opened. Workers, farmers, the poor, and the unemployed were embittered by their failure to secure a just share of the productivity of the new industrial age. And the upper classes feared their rising anger.

The Republican convention nominated William McKinley of Ohio for president. He had been a Republican congressman for many years. Always pushing for a high tariff, he was favored by big business. His campaign was in the control of Mark Hanna, a Cleveland industrialist and financier and the first political boss to operate on a national scale.

The Democrats wrote a platform calling for free coinage of silver. It condemned the trusts and monopolies and the use of injunctions—court orders to cripple labor's attempts to organize by barring strikes and boycotts. The party nominated William Jennings Bryan of Nebraska for president, and soon after, the People's Party, too, put him at the head of their ticket. Bryan, a newspaper editor, had served two terms in Congress and was an enormously popular orator. Only thirty-six now, he spoke for millions who had no other spokesman.

The Republicans, guided by the shrewd and unscrupulous Hanna, depicted Bryan as an "anarchist" and "revolutionary." While McKinley campaigned from his front porch in Canton, Ohio, Hanna drew on volunteers like TR to carry the message to the people.

The Republicans were panicky when they saw what huge crowds were coming out to greet Bryan. Preachers in high pulpits cried out that the Democrats' platform "was made in hell." The Republican press charged that Bryan "was the rival of every traitor in deliberate wickedness and treason to the Republic." The only way to beat Bryan, Hanna figured, was to paint him as anti-American, even anti-Christ. He asked TR to speak wherever Bryan had been rousing the greatest enthusiasm. And TR eagerly did so. In town after town in the Midwest he charged that Bryan was much like that other traitor, Jefferson Davis, who had led the South during the Civil War. He proclaimed that the honor of the nation was at stake, and that the true aim of Bryan's supporters was "revolution." He predicted civil war would come, and added: "When war does come, I shall be found at the head of my regiment. I speak with the greatest soberness when I say that the sentiment now animating a large proportion of our people can only be suppressed, as the Commune of Paris was suppressed, by taking ten or a dozen of their leaders out, standing them against a wall, and shooting them dead. I believe it will come to that. These leaders are plotting revolution and the subversion of the American republic."

What was this but demagogy? TR joined his party's leaders in whipping people up to a frenzy about the imminent danger of "revolution," a danger he himself had ridiculed as nonsense. It was pure—or rather impure!—politics, designed to destroy the opposition by blinding the public to the real issues.

Party chairman Hanna raised huge sums from corporations, banks, and insurance companies to finance the campaign. His scare tactics opened plenty of fat purses. More than 120 million leaflets, posters, pamphlets, badges, buttons, and books flooded the country, with frightening forecasts of disaster if Bryan should win. Working people were warned that if Bryan won, factories would close the next day. Over fourteen hundred speakers made expense-paid trips to reach every voter's ear.

TR delighted in delivering his share of the message. He had a great gift for verbal fireworks so passionately exploded that listeners easily missed the faulty reasoning or deliberate distortions behind all that verbiage. He had become so popular that when he spoke in Chicago to an audience of thirteen thousand for two hours, the next day the *Tribune* began his speech on page one, running the entire seven thousand words.

In the end Bryan got the biggest Democratic vote in history—6.5 million. But it was not enough to overcome McKinley's 7 million. The Republicans kept their control of both houses of Congress, which they had previously won in 1894. They would keep the majority they had won until 1932, the year another Roosevelt, Franklin D., would restore the Democrats to power.

Now that TR had helped put McKinley in the White House, would he get the job he wanted? The truth was, TR wasn't too happy that this particular Republican had won. Yes, he had wanted to beat Bryan at all costs. But he believed McKinley to be a weakling. Couldn't rely on him in "a serious crisis," he said, "whether it took the form of a gigantic labor riot, or danger of a foreign conflict."

As for McKinley, he wasn't too happy with the idea of appointing TR assistant secretary of the navy. Of course, he felt TR should be rewarded for his recent services. But what about that continuous uproar on the Police Board? And wasn't the man too bloody-minded? He had just published an article hailing "the rugged fighting quality" a country needed "to achieve real greatness" and had poured scorn on those who had no taste for war. McKinley thought of himself as a man of peace. And TR was a jingo, a man who believed in aggressive nationalism.

Without doubt, many recognized this trait in him. "This doctrine of jingoism, this chip-on-the-shoulder attitude," said President Eliot of Harvard, is "the attitude of a ruffian and a bully."

Ignorant of modern war, TR romanticized it. You could cite any number of conversations, letters, articles, and speeches in which TR made wild statements about the necessity of war, the good of war, the blessings of war, and the urgent need for America to expand beyond its borders to wherever its power could reach.

But more than a personality we would describe as "macho" today was behind this. TR knew from his experience out west that the great land frontier was rapidly disappearing. People with a long view were convinced that factories and farms produced more goods than Americans could consume. The only place for continual expansion of the American market-place was overseas. If prosperity was to continue, a foreign policy had to be created to achieve the constant expansion into new markets that the business system needed.

So there were economic motives, too, that led him to urge an expansionist role on the United States. Besides, TR was a staunch nationalist, bursting with patriotic pride. He put the interests of his country, as he saw them, above those of all other nations. He believed no European power had the right to be anywhere in this hemisphere. He had contempt for any leader who tried to solve international problems by any method other than superior force. To a "masterful" people, he said, "expansion is not a matter of regret, but of pride."

Like nationalists everywhere, TR was sure his country could never act unjustly or do something wrong. So whatever position America took was, of course, the right one. It followed that anyone who opposed American expansion was a moral cripple. That is why he was always calling people who differed with him "crooks!" A British journalist who reported on TR for decades said that "he honestly believes it impossible to differ with him honestly."

In the weeks following McKinley's inauguration, TR's friends lobbied hard for his appointment as assistant secretary of the navy, while others opposed it. Lodge told him the only reason for the delay in an appointment was "fear that you will want to fight somewhere, at once." That was true: the White House believed that TR would try to get the United States into a war. And the president wanted only a calm, peaceful term that would permit the country's business interests to continue their growth. The navy secretary himself, the mild John D. Long, nervously predicted that if TR gets the job, "he will dominate the Department within six months."

Finally the president went ahead with the appointment. In April 1897, TR was sworn in, at a salary of $4,500 a year.

10

AMBITIONS ABROAD

TR's return to Washington was greeted warmly by most of the press. Even Navy Secretary Long was reassured, finding TR polite, charming, and invaluable for his superior knowledge of naval affairs. TR, in turn, thought his boss "a perfect dear," and lazy enough to pretty much let TR run the show. Foreign observers, however, quaked at the prospect of TR shaping naval policy. "His extreme jingoism," said the *London Times*, "seems ominous."

TR quickly established himself as a leader among those influential figures in Washington—in government, the Congress, the press, the lobbyists—who shared his belief in America's Manifest Destiny. That ringing phrase had led to the Mexican War of 1846–1847, ending in the American acquisition of one-third of Mexico's land. Now it meant the drive to make America dominant throughout the Western Hemisphere and a world power as well by 1900.

He let the country know his goal in a speech he gave in June. It was a trumpeting call to arms, a call for the immediate buildup of the American navy. If U.S. power dominated the seas, what country would dare attempt invasion of the domain we claimed for ourselves? And flexing his muscles in his familiar way, he said, "All the great masterful races have been fighting races. . . . Cowardice in a race, as in an individual, is the unpardonable sin. . . . No triumph of peace is quite so great as the supreme triumphs of war." He used the word *war* sixty-two times in the speech, and concluded, "It is through strife, or the readiness for strife, that a nation must win greatness."

The speech, as he calculated, caused a national uproar. One wing of the press called it manly and patriotic, and claimed that it was what most Americans thought. Anti-imperialist journals criticized it for inciting citizens to war. TR wished to reshape foreign policy, and he succeeded. The peace-minded president himself sighed and said, "I believe that Roosevelt is right."

TR's ideas on foreign policy were much like those of Captain Alfred Thayer Mahan, a naval officer who had published a book in 1890 called *The Influence of Sea Power Upon History.* TR had given it a glowing review back then, for Mahan agreed with the thrust of TR's own first book, *The Naval War of 1812.* Both men believed that America needed a strong navy to protect its overseas trade, the key to national power. A great fleet, said Mahan, would need bases in the Caribbean and the Far East. He called, too, for a canal across Central America to speed trade between the East and West, and to allow America's battleships to move speedily from the Atlantic to the Pacific.

As soon as he took office, TR went to work on his and Mahan's program. They wanted the United States to annex Hawaii and to launch the project for an interoceanic canal. To protect a canal, the United States had to be supreme in the Caribbean, and that required kicking Spain out of Cuba.

The island had been a Spanish possession ever since Columbus had claimed it for Spain in 1492. In the eighteenth century a slave-based sugar plantation economy had developed. A two-year revolt against Spain had ended in 1878, with Spain guaranteeing the Cubans rights, a promise it failed to carry out. Then in 1895 a sweeping movement to overthrow Spanish rule began under José Martí, a struggle that laid waste to the countryside and cost many lives on both sides. To weaken the guerrilla forces the Spanish commander, General

Weyler, had penned up many women and children in concentration camps, where hundreds had died of starvation and disease.

There were mixed motives for intervening in Cuba. American business had made large investments there, seeking high profits from cheap labor. And farmers did well by exporting food to Cuba. Investors wanted a peaceful Cuba to ensure continued prosperity. TR and the expansionists wanted to push Spain out of the Western Hemisphere so America could make the Caribbean a U.S. lake. Many Americans, feeling great sympathy for the rebels, wished to end the suffering of the Cuban people and help them gain their independence.

While the Cuban issue was coming to a boil, Edith Roosevelt, pregnant again, stayed at Sagamore Hill with the children. TR moved in with some friends. In July he left Washington briefly to visit the family at Oyster Bay, playing with the swarm of young cousins who enjoyed visits to Oyster Bay. Among the guests were young Franklin D. Roosevelt and his cousin Eleanor Roosevelt, Elliott's orphaned daughter, toward whom TR was especially affectionate. In August TR moved his family into a rented house in Washington.

Secretary Long vacationed that month, and in his welcome absence TR began to put the navy on a wartime footing. Meanwhile, the president got the Senate to ratify a treaty annexing Hawaii. When the Japanese protested, TR told them it was none of their business.

At the same time, halfway around the world, another revolt had erupted against Spanish rule—in the Philippines. The islands had been claimed for Spain back in 1571, when Ferdinand Magellan's fleet had sailed into the archipelago. Congressmen and cabinet members talked to McKinley about taking control of the Philippines as a springboard into Asian markets if the United States went to war with Spain to end the mess in Cuba.

A powerful player in this mounting drama was the press. Until recently newspapers had been edited for a fairly limited number of educated readers. With the growth of mass educa-

★

TR served as the assistant secretary of the navy under President William McKinley, and played a significant role in putting the U.S. Navy on a wartime footing.

tion, and the invention of new printing technology, publishers could print huge numbers of papers and actual pictures of what was happening. William Randolph Hearst and Joseph Pulitzer, the new press lords, boosted their circulation enormously by lowering prices and offering something for everyone: hard news, sensational reporting of crime, society gossip, advice to working girls, household hints, and comic strips in color.

But truthful reporting was not a prime consideration. Hearst had decided, and Pulitzer soon agreed, that war would be a great circulation-builder. Competing for circulation, their newspapers exploited the troubles in Cuba, sending out reporters and artists with instructions to seek sensational news first of all. Hearst's *Journal* and Pulitzer's *World* filled their columns with lurid stories of alleged atrocities ordered by Spanish generals.

Still preferring peace to war, McKinley tried to negotiate with Spain over Cuba, and got the Spanish government to offer Cuba limited home rule. But the rebels would accept nothing short of complete independence. The worried McKinley put several battleships on ready call and sent the *Maine* to Havana on a "courtesy visit"—a display of power that pleased TR.

But now TR's intense focus on a possible war was diverted by grave trouble at home. After Edith had given birth to their fifth child, Quentin, she fell seriously ill. It took a while to discover she had a noncancerous abdominal tumor that had to be removed surgically. For weeks she lay close to death. Finally, in March, a slow recovery began.

Meanwhile the *Maine* rocked peacefully at anchor in Havana harbor. Then on the evening of February 15, 1898, an explosion shattered the forward part of the ship, and it sank rapidly into the harbor mud. At dawn a naval officer woke President McKinley with the terrible news. The toll was heavy: 266 of the 354 officers and men on board had been killed.

How had it happened? Had the Spanish blown up the ship? Had the Cuban rebels done it to provoke war with Spain? Was it an accident? Secretary Long thought the last was quite possible. Battleships in those days were badly constructed. And a number of accidental causes could have set off an explosion in a ship loaded with munitions.

The sensation-seeking press would not wait for a careful investigation. Headlines screamed, "Destruction of the *Maine* by Foul Play" and "The Warship *Maine* Was Split in Two by an Enemy's Secret Infernal Machine."

The navy began an investigation of the disaster, but before it could reach a conclusion, a war fever swept the nation.

★

"Remember the *Maine!*" was the popular outcry. Congress voted $50 million to prepare for war while McKinley assured Spain the United States had no desire to grab Cuba. We only want an armistice and certain concessions, he said. TR growled contemptuously that "McKinley has no more back-bone than a chocolate éclair." But before the navy reported that it could place no blame for the blowing up of the *Maine*, McKinley gave in to the powerful clamor both in and out of Congress for war. He called for "forcible intervention" by the United States to establish peace in Cuba. Before the end of April, the two nations were at war. It was hardly a contest between equals. Spain was almost bankrupt and its population was only 18 million as against 75 million in the United States.

TR had got what he wanted. In office just one year, he had done much to bring about this war. Not a war to annex Cuba, he assured an old friend, but one to secure the independence of the Cubans. Adding "whether they amount to much or not," a casual slur indicating his racist views.

Months before the outbreak of war TR had been dickering for a commission in the army. All along he had insisted he would fight himself. He would not be one of those "armchair and parlor jingoes who wish to see others do what we only advocate doing." He meant to practice what he preached.

As he prepared to resign his post, he felt proud that he had gotten the navy into great shape for war. In the course of doing so, he had made himself into a naval expert and pushed the advancement of naval technology far beyond what it had been. He had been foremost in championing torpedo boats and submarines, and had even foreseen someday the military use of a "flying machine" that a scientist had just been experimenting with.

The president called for 125,000 volunteers to multiply the power of the small regular army of 28,000 men. The secretary of war offered command of the First U.S. Volunteer Cavalry Regiment to TR. It would be a dream fulfilled. Back in his ranching days he had talked of leading a troop of "rough riders" into battle someday. But knowing he had no experience in military organization, he said he would serve as second in command if the top command would go to his old friend, Leonard Wood, an army surgeon with the rank of captain who had fought in the Indian wars.

As soon as the announcement of the new regiment was made, thousands of men volunteered. As always, although TR might be number two, everyone acted as though he were number one, and the outfit was quickly dubbed "Roosevelt's Rough Riders." Colonel Wood didn't mind; he set about preparing a training camp for the regiment in San Antonio, Texas.

On May 1 came stunning news: Commodore George Dewey had destroyed Spain's Asiatic Squadron in a seven-hour battle off Manila. It had cost not a single American life, while Spain suffered 381 casualties. What Dewey was doing there almost no one in Washington (but TR) knew. McKinley had given Congress four reasons for war, all focused on Cuba, none on the Philippines.

TR made a triumphant exit from the naval department, dropping his civvies for a cavalry officer's uniform tailored by Brooks Brothers. He took out life insurance and spent most of his last two weeks in Washington with his family. Edith, still recovering from her illness, feared what might happen to him in combat. But she hid her feelings from him, and on May 12 they said good-bye.

11

A SPLENDID LITTLE WAR

And so TR's glorious adventure began.

He couldn't wait to get into action. "It will be awful if we miss the fun," he said, fearing the navy might end the war too soon by sinking the enemy's Atlantic fleet. He was more than ready for combat. Because of his poor eyesight, he wasn't sure he would be able to see the enemy, and therefore had procured twelve pairs of steel-rimmed eyeglasses, which he tucked into folds of his uniform and the lining of his campaign hat.

At San Antonio he met his outfit, the First Volunteer Cavalry. They were a strangely mixed bunch—cowboys, desperadoes temporarily out of jail, bricklayers, farmhands, Ivy League graduates, polo players, steeplechase riders. As they sweated long days drilling under the Texas sun, TR tried to cozy up to them as man to man. But Colonel Wood put a quick stop to that poor example of military discipline.

A month later, the outfit sailed from Tampa to Cuba. The men were dismounted, for there had not been room on the transports for enough horses to equip TR's regiment. Nearly sick with impatience, he wanted the Rough Riders to arrive in time to earn their share of the glory. Their first duty as part of the Fifth Corps was to advance upon the Spanish at a point called Las Guásimas. After an hour's march through the jungle they were halted by the crash of rifle fire. A skirmish was on, and the men fired furiously at an enemy they could not see. In what some called an ambush, sixteen Americans were killed and fifty-two wounded. The Spanish losses were ten killed and eight wounded. The fight had little military significance, but TR was glad he had got his "first whack" at the Spaniards. A combat correspondent wrote that TR showed "the coolness, the calm judgment, the towering heroism which made him, perhaps, the most admired and best loved of all Americans in Cuba." News reports made it appear that TR's Rough Riders were the only true heroes of Las Guásimas. In New York, Republicans began to talk up TR as the best candidate for governor in September.

A week passed before TR got into another battle. In the usual rivalry between branches of the services, supplies had been neglected. With little for his regiment to eat, TR sent foragers out to buy supplies with his personal funds. On June 20 came the order for the troops to advance on Santiago, a key stronghold of the Spanish. If it could be taken, then the war would be over, and Cuba and the Western Hemisphere would be in America's hands.

On the morning of July 1 the men were ordered to capture the fortified village of El Caney and then San Juan Hill. To take the hill would open the road to Santiago. TR's men came under heavy fire from fortifications above them. They were in deep trouble, for directly in front were the Spanish gunners and behind them masses of their own troops blocked retreat down the road.

This would be a day that, as one Rough Rider said later, left TR "just revelling in victory and gore." But what really happened? First, the Rough Riders were not riding anything; they were on foot that day. Their horses had been left in Florida. And there's some confusion about the exact place of the famous charge up San Juan Hill as well as about who got up there first. The troops were mostly Regulars, with TR's men scattered among them. What TR chose to celebrate for the rest of his life had happened an hour before the final assault on San Juan Hill. A regiment of African-American Regulars had been ordered to wait at the base of Kettle Hill, a smaller rise on the way to San Juan Hill. And when TR led his men through them it precipitated a charge. But the black Regulars,

*The Rough Riders were a motley collection of
cowboys, bricklayers, college students, and ex-convicts.
Here, TR is seen standing at the center.*

too, raced up at once, in support of the Rough Riders, only
to find that the Spanish had abandoned Kettle Hill and fled
to San Juan Hill.

TR gathered his men and joined the Regulars hurrying on
under fire, but by the time they reached the top of San Juan
Hill, the enemy was in full flight. The Rough Riders' casualties
numbered eighty-nine, TR proudly noting that it was "the
heaviest loss suffered by any regiment in the cavalry division."

In years to come TR would tell the story of the charge up
San Juan Hill in great detail, leaving out all but his own part
in it. It was so obviously self-serving that the popular satirist,

Finley Peter Dunne, made great fun of him. In the following passage he has his fictional character, Mr. Dooley, who has just read TR's book, *The Rough Riders,* tell his pal Mr. Hennessey, about it:

> *"I haven't time f'r to tell ye the wurruk Tiddy did in ar-rmin' an' equippin' himself, how he fed himself, how he steadied himself in battles an' encouraged himself with a few well-chosen worruds whin th' sky was darkest. Ye'll have to take a squint into the book ye'erself to l'arn thim things."*
>
> *"I won't do it," said Mr. Hennessey. "I think Tiddy Rosenfelt is all r-right an' if he wants to blow his horn lave him do it."*
>
> *"Thrue f'r ye," said Mr. Dooley. . . . "But if I was him I'd call th' book Alone in Cubia."*

With his colossal ego, the "I" was sprinkled so heavily through TR's memoirs that, the story goes, the printer had to order a special supply of the letter. What helped build his reputation was the enthusiastic support of his friend, Richard Harding Davis. TR had carefully cultivated Davis, the most glamorous reporter of his time, and Davis's combat reports from Cuba transformed TR into a national hero.

The "splendid little war"—a memorable phrase of John Hay's—lasted only one hundred days, not counting the fighting in the Philippines: that came after. It cost the United States 385 killed in battle and 2,061 dead from "other causes," mostly from yellow fever. Whatever the losses in human life, they didn't seem to disturb TR. He boasted, "I killed a Spaniard with my own hand, like a jackrabbit." And when his brief day of battle was over, he said exultantly, "Look at those damned Spanish dead!" Years later, in a letter to a friend, he complained that "our generals . . . had to grapple with a public sentiment which screamed with anguish over the loss of a couple of thousand men . . . a sentiment of preposterous and unreasoning mawkishness."

As the siege of Santiago began, the Americans in their muddy trenches suffered more casualties from wounds, malaria, and dysentery. The Spanish fleet, trying to break out of the American naval blockade at the time, was nearly destroyed. On July 17, Spain surrendered and began to withdraw from Cuba. A few days later messages from New York poured in to TR, urging him to consider running for governor. He didn't say yes, but neither did he say no; clearly, he was available.

By now, half the Rough Riders were dead or disabled by wounds and sickness. To save lives, the army was ordered to leave Cuba at once and sail north to Montauk, Long Island. TR boarded ship, bursting with pride over his share in the victory. At last he had fought in a war and shed the enemy's blood. He wrote Lodge that he hoped the senator would use his influence to get him a Congressional Medal of Honor, for "I think I have earned it."

As Spain gave up Cuba, America occupied the island and later got from Spain the Caribbean island of Puerto Rico, the Pacific island of Guam, and all the Philippines. When Hawaii was annexed, it set a powerful precedent for the United States to build a "legal" empire in the Pacific and to establish a growing political and economic stranglehold over Cuba and Puerto Rico. These gains were much greater than the original aim of winning independence for Cuba. But they were exactly what TR and the expansionists desired. They had acted on the humane impulse to help the suffering Cubans and had turned it into something very different.

Out of that war came a broad anti-imperialist movement. When rumors spread that the McKinley administration planned to take over the Philippines, Boston reformers organized the Anti-Imperialist League to prevent the war from being "perverted into a war of conquest." Leaders from a great many fields supported the league—writers like Mark Twain and William Dean Howells, feminists, educators, lawyers, urban reformers, blacks, trade unionists. They organized public meetings, mobilized supporters, and wrote articles, pamphlets, and books to make a strong case against McKinley's decision to seize the Philippines as a base from which to expand American power into Asia. They gave many arguments, sometimes conflicting, but at the heart of their opposition was the belief that imperialism was just plain wrong. It would corrupt our constitutional principles and cripple our democratic freedoms.

TR didn't see it that way. He proclaimed the war with Spain "the most absolutely righteous foreign war" of the nineteenth century. He shared with other imperialists the belief that people of Anglo-Saxon descent were superior to the peoples over whom America was extending its rule. A French writer said that the Anglo-Saxon "race" was destined to rule the world, and TR agreed. He endorsed the concept of white superiority. To him even the Chinese, with their ancient culture, were an inferior race. When the annexation of Hawaii was being debated, he said that the United States ought to take the islands "in the interests of the white race." His writings were laced with references to the "race foe" and the "dangerous alien."

Unlike many racists of his time, he didn't think "backward people" would always be inferior. Every people could progress, he said, however slowly. He liked to think that he judged individuals on their own merit, not as members of a race or class or nation. Any person of achievement he admired and treated as an equal.

When it came to foreign policy, he would argue that the spread of Anglo-Saxon power would bring world peace and the spread of civilization. So when America began to extend its empire, he justified expansion on the ground that the United States was serving the "backward" peoples. Like many Americans at that time, he believed that white people must bear the burden of civilizing the colonial peoples—if necessary, against their will. It was for their own good that we performed this "great and righteous task."

Another chapter in the Roosevelt epic was about to begin. In mid-April he was mustered out at Montauk Point. A crowd had gathered at the pier to watch the troopship bearing the

★

Rough Riders come in. "Roosevelt! Roosevelt!" they shouted. "Hurrah for Teddy and the Rough Riders!" While the survivors of his regiment looked terribly sick and emaciated, TR radiated good health. Three months in Cuba had left him feeling "disgracefully well." he said. Talking to the press, he patted his heavy revolver and told them, "When I took it to Cuba I made a vow to kill at least one Spaniard with it and I did!"

Home so soon after the splendid little war, he found himself the most famous man in America.

12

FROM GOVERNOR TO VICE PRESIDENT

Even before the Rough Riders were discharged from service at Montauk, TR was deep in politicking for the nomination as governor of New York. For that, he needed the support of Senator Thomas C. Platt, boss of the state's Republican Party, and the chief voice of the corporations at Albany. Platt wasn't sure where TR's sympathies lay. Would this Rough Rider come down on the side of business—or of labor? But the party needed a fresh face badly. It had been tainted with charges of corruption. Only the glamour of the hero of San Juan Hill might win for them this time.

And then there were the reformers. They also wanted TR; they hoped he would run on their independent ticket. He would strengthen their tiny party, cripple Platt's political machine, and might even win.

TR knew Platt wanted a guarantee of good behavior, meaning that TR would do as the party desired. Yes, I'll run on your ticket, he said, and will work with the organization on appointments and legislation. But he added, in pious tones, that he would not violate the standards of general decency. To which Platt responded, *he* can have the Ten Commandments so long as *we* win.

To the Independents, TR said that while he would head the Republican ticket as a party regular, he would welcome Independent endorsement too. He played the Independents on his line like a skilled fisherman, letting them build support for him among people who were sick of the old party machines.

And then, at the last minute, he cut the line, refusing to allow his name to be placed on their ticket. Their leader, John Jay Chapman, an old friend, was furious at this betrayal. TR was denounced as a "broken-backed, half-good man" and the puppet of Boss Platt. Chapman never spoke to him again.

TR thought of himself as a reformer, but as a practical politician, too. To get along, you have to go along—an old political axiom. He campaigned very effectively, making promises to the Irish and the Germans, the Jews and the Catholics, labor and other groups.

The Democrats' man was Augustus van Wyck, a personally honest, though obscure, judge. His nomination had been engineered by the head of Tammany Hall just as TR's had been by Boss Platt.

TR toured the state, drawing great crowds. He made patriotism the keynote of the campaign, to the point that one critic said, "He thinks he's the American flag." Seven Rough Riders in uniform toured with him, one of them blowing a charge on a cavalry bugle at every stop, just before TR spoke. Even when he said nothing, remarked an observer, "The man's presence was everything. It was electrical, magnetic." He would brag about the glorious victory of his Rough Riders in Cuba and denounce the horrid evils of government by Tammany. Like the true political animal he had become, he loved every minute of it. And he discovered the power he had to sway great crowds.

But even so, he won the governorship only by a narrow margin—18,000 votes out of some 1.3 million cast. The Republicans' reputation had soured so badly that the party would probably have lost if it had not been for the sheer force of TR's personality.

Waiting to take office in January 1899, TR began dictating his war memoirs, first for serial publication in a magazine and then to be issued as a book called *The Rough Riders*. He also gave eight lectures at Harvard, by these ventures adding handsomely to the family income. As governor he would draw a salary of $10,000 a year. For the first time in their twelve-year marriage, he and Edith could stop worrying about their finances.

The family moved into the musty old Governor's Mansion in Albany. Edith tried to make it livable by bringing in some of their own furniture and decorating the walls with paintings from home. They found space for a schoolroom and a gymnasium, too, as much for TR himself as for the children, as this big eater had put on far too much weight.

Now TR's real test began. He had to keep his promise to Boss Platt—to reward the faithful with jobs and to consult on legislative proposals. He proved how skillful he could be in getting around the resistance to change by the machines of both old parties. And substantial changes there had to be if he was to be able to live with his conscience and build a political future.

He was careful to provide Platt and his lieutenants with enough patronage to keep them happy. This, while insisting on the appointment of the best talents they could agree on for state jobs. In just as careful a way, TR offered a legislative program. He tried nothing radical, going by precedent, and always consulted Platt first. If Platt opposed a suggestion, and they could not reach a compromise, TR usually dropped the proposal. Still, at times he pushed hard against Platt's will, but only when he could appeal over the boss's head to the state's voters and then, with their support, force the legislature to enact his bill.

He learned how to use public relations to manipulate the machine and realize his goals. The result was, as he put it, "a hodgepodge compounded of the ideal and the practicable." And in his modest way, he added that this was "simply the combination which made Washington and Lincoln great powers for good."

What did he accomplish in his term? (Only two years in that era.) Made conscious of labor's power by the great upheavals of recent times, he tried to win labor's support by offering bills to meet some of its needs. He was the first governor to visit sweatshops (with his old friend Jacob Riis), and he got

★

the legislature to pass a law regulating them. Years earlier, while in the assembly, he had fought hard against an eight-hour law for workers on government contracts. But now, more sensitive to labor's needs, he signed just such a bill.

He increased the number of factory inspectors, created a Tenement-House Commission whose findings led to improved housing conditions, and put through protective safety measures for women and children who worked.

While protecting labor, the farmers, and the consumers, he disciplined business, too. One of his proposals that met stiff resistance from both parties was to make the wealthy men who owned franchises pay the state taxes for the profitable privileges given them. He won. It was, he said, the beginning of an effort "to make the great corporations really responsible to popular wish and governmental command." He spoke openly of "the combination of business with politics and the judiciary which has done so much to enthrone privilege in the economic world." He also had a strong civil service law passed, the best of any state in the nation.

TR was always a staunch defender of the rights of property and of the authority of the state to protect those rights. The state should act justly, however, and try to help improve the conditions of people by social legislation. Still, if labor showed any independent power, especially in the form of a strike, he could blow up. (He had shown that early on in his violent reactions to the news of labor troubles.) As governor, too, he displayed a "trigger-like willingness to use troops," wrote the labor historian Howard Hurwitz. "His mind was a single track when it came to strikes, and that track always carried troops to the scene of the dispute," as it did in strikes at the Croton Aqueduct and in Buffalo.

In his two years in office TR advanced the cause of conservation. He looked to experts for advice on legislative proposals, and in his messages and speeches educated the public on the need to preserve our natural resources. He was the first governor of New York, or of any state, said the biologist Paul Cutright, "to speak out so fully and so forthrightly about the related topics of forest preservation, forest fires, flooding, stream pollution, soil erosion, reservoirs, illegal hunting, wildlife controls, and watersheds."

In years to come New Yorkers would benefit mightily from his pioneering environmental policies. And other states, too, began to follow his recommended measures for protecting their own natural resources.

TR introduced new methods to reach the public with his messages. Today every politician has a highly professional publicity operation. But TR was the first governor of New York to hold press conferences regularly. Twice a day, whenever he was in Albany, he would meet reporters in his office and for fifteen minutes take questions. He would soften up the reporters with jokes and gossip and then provide inside tips and clues to policy. His main concern, he said, was to arouse the voters through the press to the most threatening of "the great fundamental questions looming before us"—the powerful link between politics and big business.

If the greedy corporations were allowed to seize and control the creative forces of society, he believed civilization would be in danger. He recognized that the rich were getting richer and the poor poorer, and that masses of people lived desperate lives in the ghettos of the big cities. "My own belief," he wrote a friend, "is that we shall have to pay far more attention to . . . tremendous problems . . . of the relation of labor to capital."

He had made at least a beginning with his winning fight for the basic principle of taxing franchise privileges. He wished the country had a more powerful and visionary leader than McKinley to put through similar laws on a national scale. McKinley was likely to win a second term in 1900. But already there was talk of Roosevelt for president in 1904. His friend Senator Lodge urged him to consider a vice-presidential nomination in 1900. That would be the smoothest path to the top of the ticket four years later. But TR had trouble picturing himself in an essentially do-nothing job. No, he said, the vice presidency was "about the last thing for which I would care."

★

*As governor of New York, Teddy Roosevelt held
daily press briefings with Albany correspondents.*

Meanwhile, with Albany not in session, he began work
on a biography of Oliver Cromwell, the English general and
statesman of the seventeenth century. It took him only one
month to dictate the 63,000 words, talking from notes, and
another month for revisions. In between paragraphs on Cromwell, he would dictate official letters as governor. This book,
like some of his many others, hasn't stood up. But it reveals
how he saw himself in relation to other great political figures.

Nearly forty-one, with a happy marriage, many children,
a livable income, and the leadership of the largest state in the
Union, what more could he hope for? Only the presidency.

That would put him at the pinnacle of power, a height where *his* will would be supreme.

Of course McKinley already had a vice president, Garret A. Hobart, who liked the office and had no intention of leaving it. But then, in late November 1899, Hobart died. And that changed the picture. Someone had to replace him on the ticket. Boss Platt thought TR was just the man. So, ironically, did the franchise holders, who hated the tax that he had imposed on them. Rumors flew that TR's "altruism"— which to Platt meant communism—would lead to more laws limiting what the corporations could do. The best way to get rid of the man would be to kick him upstairs into the vice president's seat.

It worked. McKinley, after resisting at first, finally agreed to accept TR as his running mate. At the party's convention in Philadelphia, TR was chosen by unanimous vote. His nomination had been engineered by Platt and the party bosses, a fact TR never admitted. While glad to have TR out of the way, they prayed McKinley would live out his second term of four years.

Again Bryan was the Democrats' presidential candidate. As in 1896, McKinley stayed home, letting TR stump the country to take on Bryan. Bryan campaigned against the Republicans' imperialist policy. Using the annexation of the Philippines, he condemned the reported atrocities by the American occupation forces and demanded that America withdraw its troops. TR's reply was to proclaim that the U.S. victory over Spain had won the world's respect and brought prosperity to all.

He made no apology for expansionism. On the contrary he said: "Of course our whole national history has been one of expansion. . . . That the barbarians recede or are conquered, with the attendant fact that peace follows their retrogression or conquest, is due solely to the power of the mighty civilized races which have not lost the fighting instinct, and which by their expansion are gradually bringing peace into the red wastes where the barbarian peoples of the world hold sway."

He denounced Bryan's proposals for an inheritance tax and a graduated income tax. But he cautioned that the trusts needed to be watched, and their profits taxed. Giving hundreds of speeches in twenty-four states, he traveled 21,000 miles, reaching 3 million people. All this while McKinley remained invisible. It made people think TR was the presidential candidate. He wasn't running, he was galloping, observed Mr. Dooley.

The Republicans won easily, in their greatest victory since Grant won in 1872. They beat Bryan by nearly a million votes. TR saw it as public approval for the new role of the United States as the leading world power, a victory he could personally take credit for. And now he had become the front runner for the presidential nomination come 1904.

He and the president were sworn in on March 4, 1901. But TR's new duties amounted to almost nothing. The vice president, as one joker said, has only two duties: to preside over the Senate and to inquire about the president's health each morning. His first role lasted only four days. The Senate approved of presidential appointments quickly, and then adjourned until December. The restless TR chafed at having nothing to do.

Yet he enjoyed the idle days ahead. The family summered at Sagamore Hill, with TR spending the days riding and rowing with Edith, playing with the children, chopping trees, and in the evening reading by the fireside. In the fall they were back in Washington, living in a large rented house on Connecticut Avenue.

TR and McKinley went on separate speaking tours early in September. While TR was meeting with a group of Vermont sportsmen on September 6, the president was ending a visit to the Pan American Exposition at Buffalo. He was greeting hundreds of visitors in the Temple of Music, shaking hands with them as they filed by. Just before the reception was to end, a young Polish-American anarchist named Leon Czolgosz came up, extending his left hand because his right was wrapped in a handkerchief as though injured. McKinley reached for the left hand, but Czolgosz suddenly raised his bandaged right hand, shoved it against the president's chest, and fired two quick shots from a concealed revolver.

No one knew how badly the president was hurt. TR was telephoned the shocking news and hurried to Buffalo. When optimistic reports came from the doctors, TR left to join his family in the Adirondacks. But on September 13 the president got much worse. Telegrams reached TR, calling on him to rush back to Buffalo. Before he could arrive, McKinley died in the early hours of September 14. He was the third president to be assassinated while in office.

The next day TR took the presidential oath of office in a private home, with most members of the cabinet present. Then he said: "I am at one mind with the members of the cabinet. I will show the people at once that the administration of the government will not falter in spite of the terrible blow. I wish to say that it shall be my aim to continue, absolutely unbroken, the policy of President McKinley for the peace, the prosperity, and the honor of our beloved country."

He had been vice president for only six months. Now, at forty-two, he had become the youngest president in history.

13

IN THE WHITE HOUSE

T R's arrival in the White House marked a dramatic change in American history. Here was the youngest man who had ever held that office. Here was an aristocrat, a Harvard graduate, a man who read books, even wrote books, and traveled to Europe, a bird-watcher, a Rough Rider, and the most energetic politician who had ever run for office. Here was a Republican from New York, the great city many Americans detested and feared, yet a man with extraordinary national appeal. Here was a man who loved power and would exercise it in a way few presidents before him had ever done.

Yes, he loved being president and wasn't ashamed to show it. When he took office on McKinley's death, "the whole country was in mourning," said Lincoln Steffens, "and no doubt the President felt he should hold himself down; he didn't; he tried to, but his joy showed in every word and movement."

People could not resist his colorful personality, the youthful, almost childlike quality he had. An English friend said of him, "You must always remember the President is about six." TR was the first president to be affectionately referred to by his initials. He startled visitors by making them take long walks with him in the woods around Washington. When two British diplomats came by in formal dress, they found themselves wading through a duck pond with the president as he kept chatting away. The French ambassador never forgot the time that TR walked him to the bank of a stream too deep to be forded and, stripping off his own clothes, had the poor dignitary do the same, so they could swim to the other side.

Newspaper reporters ate up such happenings, and their readers delighted in hearing of them. The press could count on the president doing or saying something newsworthy almost every day. It made covering the White House a cinch and a pleasure, and of course TR was rarely criticized by them. The president was like Niagara Falls, said one observer, a great wonder of nature.

And like the waters of Niagara, his talk gushed endlessly. Senator Joseph B. Foraker recalled that he rarely went to the White House unless he had a question of policy difference to discuss. But, he said, "I never found that either agreeable or profitable. . . . The President in such conversations always 'had the drop on me'; that being President, courtesy required me to defer to him, with the result that he generally did all the discussing, and I came away at the end of his conversation with the feeling that I had not accomplished anything."

One of TR's biographers, Edmund Morris, has captured TR as talker:

> *Roosevelt is not a twitcher—in moments of repose he is almost cataleptically still—but when talking his entire body mimes the rapidity of his thoughts. The right hand shoots out, bunches into a fist, and smacks into the left palm; the heels click together, the neck bulls forward; then, in a spasm of amusement, his face contorts, his head tosses back, spectacle-ribbons flying, and he shakes from head to foot with laughter. A moment later he is listening with passionate concentration, crouching forward and massaging the speaker's shoulder as if to wring more information out of him. Should he hear something not to his liking, he recoils as if stung, and the blood rushes to his face.*

The legal scholar Felix Frankfurter, adviser to presidents and later a Supreme Court justice, spoke of how "boisterous a creature" TR was, "a man with so much animal zest, so much

★

horsepower." He called him "a good administrator, creative in that most difficult of arts, the art of government." The British historian Hugh Brogan believed TR to be "the ablest man to sit in the White House since Lincoln; the most vigorous since Jackson; the most bookish since John Quincy Adams."

All through his years in the White House, TR carried a revolver with him wherever he went, even into states where possession was illegal. And he slept with it beside his pillow. (Not to wonder: hadn't three presidents been murdered in his lifetime?)

With his great flair for the dramatic, he took naturally to the role of the ruler as performer. TR put on a great show. He was the first political leader in the twentieth century to do that. Stalin later did it, too, and Hitler and Mussolini and Franklin Roosevelt and Winston Churchill.

Now he had the world's biggest stage to act on. How he would perform, no one knew. His first official words had been that he would "continue absolutely unbroken" the policies of McKinley. That gave some comfort to big business. But they wondered nervously what the new and untried president would do. Mark Hanna was chief boss of the Republican Party. He believed that whatever was good for the big corporations was good for the country. When he heard the news of McKinley's assassination, he exclaimed, "And now look—that damned cowboy is President of the United States!"

But other conservatives said not to worry. They had noticed that TR's official actions as New York governor were quite moderate. His talk might be big, but his actions were small. And he had always been loyal to the party. Besides, both houses of Congress were controlled by solid Republican majorities, almost wholly conservative. They took for granted that wealth should rule the country. And since industrialists were the greatest producers of wealth, their interests must be protected above all else.

Once TR grabbed the reins, there was an immediate change in the way things were done. Everything speeded up.

TR had a huge appetite for work and expected everyone else to work as hard. Administrative supervision was much tighter. Politicians were summoned to the White House at all hours of the day. Strange people showed up at the president's dining table: labor leaders, naturalists, professors, poets, prizefighters.

In his first message to Congress, in December 1901, there were no fireworks. Just a hint of trouble. He blasted assassins and anarchists, pressed for the expansion of foreign markets, and asked for restrictive tests for would-be immigrants and a large national program of conservation and reclamation.

Acting cautiously, he faced both ways on the issue of the giant business combines. First, he said that their growth was a "natural" thing. But then he added that the old laws and customs regarding the piling up of wealth and its distribution were "no longer sufficient" and went on to mention the "real and grave evils" of large industry.

If TR hedged his policy proposals with "on the one hand" and "on the other hand" phrases, it was because he realized that unless he cooperated with the conservatives dominating Congress, he would get little or no action from them. Besides, a head-on collision with the leadership would endanger his nomination and election in 1904. That concern never left his mind.

Early in 1902 the blow fell upon big business. The attorney general announced that at the president's request he was about to prosecute the Northern Securities Company for violating the Sherman Anti-Trust Act of 1890. The NSC was a giant combine, or holding company, that Pierpont Morgan, the country's financial superpower, had just set up to eliminate the competition among three major railroads by creating a transportation monopoly. The news of the prosecution shocked the business world. So little had been done to enforce the Sherman law that it was ignored or forgotten. And hadn't decisions of the Supreme Court held that there was nothing wrong with such business combines?

Morgan thought that this was very unfair of the president. Why hadn't TR told him in advance of his intention? They could have worked something out. So he left his Wall Street office to meet with the president in the White House. "If we've done something wrong," he told TR, "send your man to my man and they can fix it up."

"That can't be done," said the president. Besides, the government didn't want to "fix it up." It wanted to stop illegal mergers. Well, then, said Morgan, are you going to attack any of my other interests? He was thinking especially of the giant U.S. Steel Corporation, which he had recently organized. "Certainly not," replied TR. "Unless we find out that in any case they have done something that we regard as wrong."

Morgan left the White House, hot with anger. The president was not behaving as one gentleman should to another. He was acting instead like a politician, upsetting the projects of good, honest men in order to win public favor.

TR was angry, too, at the arrogance of men like Morgan. He believed that "in no other country was such power held by the men who had gained these fortunes. The government [was] practically impotent. Of all forms of tyranny the least attractive and the most vulgar is the tyranny of mere wealth, the tyranny of a plutocracy."

Of course TR was taking advantage of the shift in public opinion that had begun in recent years. The suffering caused by the depression of the 1890s, the rising prices brought about by the monopolies, and a recent steel strike in which the U.S. Steel Corporation had refused to deal with union labor and had broken the strike—all these had made people think. Many Americans sympathized with the strikers when they learned for the first time how the steel industry had made its workers sweat through twelve-hour days.

Wall Street lawyers felt the suit against the NSC would be defeated. But they guessed wrong. The change in the climate of opinion had influenced the courts too. Two years later, in May 1904, the Supreme Court reversed its former position on such holding companies. It ruled NSC illegal and ordered its dissolution.

One editorial declared, rather optimistically, that it was

Although the Sherman Anti-Trust Act was established
to limit the growth of large corporations, many felt that
Roosevelt was inconsistent in the enforcement of this law.

no longer a question as to whether the corporations ruled over the people or the people over the corporations. Over the next years, TR's administration started similar actions against forty-four corporations. They had grown frighteningly in numbers and power. Major consolidations took place in oil, tobacco, copper, telephone, telegraph, gas, electric power and light, chemicals, beef. . . . TR's pressure upon them won him the name of the "trustbuster."

But don't mistake his intentions. He was never out to destroy the giant corporations. He believed that their growth was natural, inevitable, even beneficial. You couldn't hold back their rise any more than you could turn back the Mississippi spring floods. But, he said, you can "regulate and control them by levees." We draw the line against misconduct, not against wealth, he said.

To do this he went to the courts and not to Congress—and for good reason. He knew the conservative Congress would never pass laws that controlled the corporations. With that path to effective legislations blocked, the only way to tame the trusts was by enforcing the existing antitrust laws.

TR's next move was to establish a new Department of Commerce and Labor and, within it, a Bureau of Corporations. Its job was to conduct investigations and issue reports on those corporations that were not being run properly. If "wrongdoing" was found, the bureau was to notify the business executives. If they didn't correct the errors themselves, their corporation could be broken up under the Sherman Act. The president was developing a two-pronged method: publicity and prosecution.

By the time his second term began, TR felt that federal regulation was the only practical way to tackle the problems created by the growth of the combines and monopolies. In 1906 he had Congress pass the Hepburn Act. It increased the powers of the Interstate Commerce Commission so that it could inspect the business records of railroads to check on their profits. It could also fix the maximum rates the railroads could charge for passenger and freight traffic.

What were the results of TR's antitrust campaign? While it was a technical success, the prosecution of the giant corporate monopoly of the NSC did not restore competition to the railroads. Nor did the court's decision lead to criminal prosecution of the railroad executives, which should have happened under the requirements of the Sherman Act. In no instance did his administration bring a criminal indictment against any corporation official. TR would claim that "one of the great achievements of my administration" was to hold "the most powerful men in the country" accountable before the law. As it turned out, not many, and not by much. Picture the Antitrust Division of the Justice Department, with a staff of four lawyers and five secretaries, combating the combined might of scores of giant corporations. Pathetic. The historian Richard Hofstadter wrote, "There was a hundred times more noise than accomplishment" in TR's regime. TR himself admitted privately as he left the White House that "As a matter of fact, I have let up in every case where I have had any possible excuse for so doing."

14

STRIKERS AND
ROLLER SKATERS

The great industrial trusts didn't like government intervention in their affairs. Nor did they like organized labor interfer-
ing with their methods of production. They resented unions
and collective bargaining. They felt that it was their sacred
right to make technological changes, set wages and hours, and
hire and fire workers.

The coalfields were the worst example of capital's arrogance toward labor. The savage abuse of miners had long been
comparable to the horrors of slavery. In the two years prior to
TR's presidency, eight hundred miners had been killed in
accidents. This was long before the passage of workmen's
compensation laws. A young miner named John Mitchell had
organized the United Mine Workers union, giving the workers
hope that their lives would someday improve.

In 1900 most miners received wages of around $350 to
$450 a year. They had been given no increases since 1880. In
the great Pennsylvania coalfields, Morgan, Vanderbilt, and
other financial lords had squeezed out the smaller operators
and added most of the anthracite mines to their railroad empires. When reformers questioned how workers could exist on
the low wages paid them, the mine operator George F. Baer
said, mining is "a business . . . not a religious, sentimental,
or academic proposition." Meanwhile, keeping wages low, he
raised the price of coal per ton.

The miners lived in company towns, where their lives were
completely controlled by the corporation. Their children, said
the labor leader Samuel Gompers, were "brought into the

world by a company doctor, lived in a company house or hut, were nurtured by the company store . . . [and] laid away in a company grave."

Reaching the point of desperation, 140,000 miners, demanding a wage raise, a shorter working day, and fair play in the weighing of coal, rose in May 1902 in a great strike. It threatened the country with an acute coal shortage for the coming winter. Month after month went by with the owners making no move to settle the strike. The union appealed to Morgan to negotiate. No, he said, he would not "interfere," and he ordered the miners back to work. "Then, and not till then," he said, "will we agree to talk about concessions."

After six months of coal shortage and suffering, groups of businessmen in the coal region urged TR to intervene. Was Morgan greater than the people? Was he mightier than the government? He would bring about ruin, riot, and bloodshed, they predicted.

Public opinion swung toward the miners as people saw that the union was willing to arbitrate the issues while the owners stubbornly refused. George Baer stuck to his guns. "God in His Infinite Wisdom had given control of the property interests of the country" exclusively to the Christian gentlemen who now directed the nation's corporations, he said. Such a statement, sounding like a proclamation of the divine right of kings, angered even conservatives. A few of the leading newspapers suggested it might be time for government to assume ownership of the mines, while others demanded compulsory arbitration. Some editors wrote that the rights and needs of the public welfare were superior to all considerations of private property.

Breaking with precedent—earlier presidents had called out the army and driven strikers back to work at bayonet's point—TR stepped into the dispute. He summoned both sides to a meeting in Washington. It was a bitter session, with George Baer's insolent behavior making the president furious. TR suggested bringing in a third party to resolve the dispute— the public. John Mitchell said the strikers would accept a presidential commission to judge the issues, and would accept its decision as final, whatever the ruling. But Baer called the miners criminals, accused them of sabotage, even though this strike had been unusually peaceful, and criticized the president for negotiating with these "fomentors of anarchy."

Finally, several days later, under pressure from the Republican boss Mark Hanna and Morgan, who realized how stupidly Baer was acting, the coal operators agreed to negotiation. A seven-man commission studied the issues, and in March 1903 awarded a 10 percent wage increase and the correction of certain abuses. But recognition of the miners union was denied. The agreement was to last for three years.

TR lamented the "folly of the very rich men." They did not see that the attitude of the coal companies was accelerating the rise of radicalism. He understood the mood of the people and used his political skill to drain their anger into the channels of moderate action. He was the first president to call representatives of both capital and labor to the White House during a labor dispute and to use the influence of the government to obtain a negotiated settlement.

TR was willing to meet with union leaders to consider their point of view. He believed working people had a right to join unions without interference from employers. But he also believed in the "open shop." He opposed boycotts by labor. While he spoke out against the use of force by labor during strikes, he refused to condemn publicly the use of illegal force by the corporations. In essence, his was the paternalistic view of a man occupying a superior station in life. As he once said, "The friends of property must realize that the surest way to provoke an explosion of wrong and injustice is to be shortsighted, narrow-minded, greedy and arrogant, and to fail to show in actual work that here in this republic it is peculiarly incumbent upon the man with whom things have prospered to be in a certain sense the keeper of his brother with whom life has gone hard."

Life in the White House wasn't all business. It's hard to think of the Executive Mansion as the country's most expensive example of public housing—a house where both business and family life went on: "It's like living over the store," said Mrs. Roosevelt.

The "storekeeper," TR, drew a presidential salary of $50,000 a year and sizable funds for upkeep, fuel, lighting, stationery, and so forth. As soon as they moved in, Mrs. Roosevelt decided the mansion was so shabby and tasteless that it had to be renovated. TR prevailed upon Congress to vote half a million dollars to carry out Edith's wishes. A new West Wing of executive offices was built, freeing the vast space above the East Room for Edith to create two suites of guest rooms and to provide better quarters for her own large brood. Ugly furnishings put in by previous presidents were stripped away, a stairway removed, the state dining room enlarged so that it could seat about one hundred, and new furniture and cabinetwork installed. Lighting fixtures, heating systems, and plumbing were modernized. Outside, the gardens were newly landscaped, a new entry built, and elegant cast-iron gates erected.

First Ladies had usually held weekly receptions at the White House. Edith turned them into musicales, preceded by a dinner for a select group of about twenty. Hundreds of other guests joined them after dinner, to hear performances by great artists.

When the new West Wing was finished, TR found ample space for his office and his staff of thirty-eight assistants, as well as the press corps. A *New York Times* reporter who covered the White House during TR's time, left this account of the president's working habits:

> *Here, in the Cabinet Room, those who call to see the President are usually received by him, from 10:00 A.M. to 1:30 P.M. Between ten and twelve Senators and Representatives have the entrée without the need of an appointment. Others must make an appointment with Secretary Loeb. Sometimes a score of people will be in the Cabinet Room at one time, and the President goes from one to another,*

★

making the circle of the room half a dozen times in a morning, always speaking with great animation, gesturing freely, and in fact talking "with his whole being, mouth, eyes, forehead, cheeks and neck all taking their mobile parts." He stands for the most part as rigid as a soldier on parade, chin in, chest out, the line from the back of the head falling straight as a plumb line to the heels. . . . When the President sits, it may be on the divan or on the Cabinet table, he is very much at his ease, and half the time one foot is curled up under him. Curiously, whenever he tucks one foot under him, his visitor is very likely to do the same thing.

A hundred times a day the President will laugh, and, when he laughs, he does it with the same energy with which he talks. It is usually a roar of laughter, and it comes nearly every five minutes. His face grows red with merriment, his eyes nearly close, his utterance becomes choked and sputtery and falsetto, and sometimes he doubles up with paroxysm. You don't smile with Mr. Roosevelt; you shout with laughter with him, and then you shout again while he tries to cork up more laughs and sputters: "Come, gentlemen, let us be serious."

Talking, writing, dictating—the outpouring of TR's energy never lets up. He wore out secretaries with relentless hours of dictation, not only on official matters but for his private correspondence, his articles, his book reviews. The staff had to work in relays to keep up with the endless flow of words.

Self-centered as he could be, he still had to know what everyone else was thinking, especially of him. He tuned in to every nuance of the press's coverage, pro and con. One assistant skimmed hundreds of newspapers every day and underlined for TR's attention every item reflecting how the country felt. Edith, too, alerted him to whatever she thought was significant.

With a strong sense of the place presidential wives held, Edith had her architects design a spacious corridor for a First

*The Roosevelt family in 1907. From left to right are
Kermit, Archie, TR, Ethel, Edith, Quentin, and Ted.*

Ladies Gallery. Dominating the busts and portraits that lined the gallery walls was a new painting of Edith, a gift from the French people.

Not since the Lincoln family, with its ebullient boys, had occupied the White House had the press had such entertaining copy to send out. The Roosevelt children kept adding pets to their extraordinary menagerie, just as their father had done when he was a boy. There was Emily Spinach, the green snake; Loretta, the parrot; Eli, the blue macaw; Tom Quartz, the kitten; and a kangaroo rat who liked to be fed sugar cubes at the breakfast table.

There was little peace or quiet in the Roosevelt White House. The kids made a roller-skating rink out of the new East Room because its parquet floor was so irresistibly smooth. Quentin liked to drop odd objects from his upstairs window onto the heads of innocent passersby. None of the children would take orders from anyone. And Edith could not get their father to intervene. He believed "children should be given entire freedom for their own inclinations."

In the first summer of his presidency, the family vacationed at Sagamore Hill. The press followed them, of course, despite TR's plaintive protests that he ought to be left alone at least on holiday, like any family man. They reported that he camped out with his children on remote islands, chopped down trees, labored on the grounds, and galloped across country.

Then, on September 4, 1902, the press had frightening news. TR had gone on a speaking tour of New England. In Pittsfield, Massachusetts, riding in a carriage drawn by four horses, his driver suddenly veered across the trolley tracks without noticing a trolley speeding down on them. The trolley slammed into them almost broadside, throwing the Secret Service agent—a friend beloved by the children—to the tracks, killing him almost instantly. One of the horses was killed, too. TR was hurled out of the carriage, landing about thirty feet away. He was badly bruised and shaken, but

First he chops down a few trees.

Then takes a cross-country canter.

And a twenty-minute brisk walk.

After which he gives the children a wheel-barrow ride.

He then rests for a moment.

By which time he is ready for breakfast.

A typical "day at rest" at Sagamore Hill, satirized by the artist

bystanders helped him up. A few hours later he gave his scheduled talk in nearby Lenox and then continued on his tour, ending up in Bridgeport, Connecticut. Edith hurried across the Long Island Sound to meet him there, finding him with a bruised cheek and a badly scraped leg. It had been a miraculous escape. If the trolley had struck the carriage only a foot or two from where it did, it would have been the end of him. As it was, the leg injury turned out not to be minor. It abscessed, requiring surgery, and would give him trouble for the rest of his life.

15

BOOKER T. WASHINGTON
AND BROWNSVILLE

What happened when TR invited the black leader Booker T. Washington to dine with him in the White House was a sign of how deeply divided the nation was over the issue of racial equality. When TR issued the invitation, there were nine million African-Americans. Nine out of every ten still lived in the South. About half of the employed blacks were in agriculture, and a third, most of them women, were in domestic or personal service. Black men who had no work, or very little, were common. Probably one black in every two could not read or write.

In 1901, at the time of the invitation, Washington, the founder and the head of Tuskegee Institute in Alabama, was the most prominent African-American. He had built his school as a training ground for African-Americans to work with their hands, rather than to prepare them for professional careers. He knew what narrow limits whites placed on black aspirations. In 1895 he had given a major speech in Atlanta, voicing a policy that overnight would make him the most famous African-American in the country and the most influential among powerful whites. He preached that blacks must accommodate to whites' refusal to permit people of color to become anything more than menials. Whites, he said, would find his people "the most patient, faithful, law-abiding and unresentful people that the world has seen." In return for economic opportunity, he implied, blacks would accept for the time being an inferior social status.

TR at Carnegie Hall with Booker T. Washington, the
founder of the Tuskegee Institute. When Teddy Roosevelt
invited Washington to dine with him at the White House,
it ignited a firestorm of angry editorials.

That seemed to endorse the doctrine of "separate but equal." And the next year, the Supreme Court of the United States endorsed it, too. In the famous *Plessy* v. *Ferguson* decision, the justices enshrined as law the position that "separate but equal" public facilities were constitutional. The ruling would remain law until 1954, when the Warren Court overturned it.

So when TR sat down to break bread with the black leader, it ignited a firestorm of protest. "The most damnable outrage" and "a crime equal to treason" were some of the milder editorial protests. Was the president trying to restore the "dreadful" years of Reconstruction? (That brief time after the Civil War when blacks and whites in the South lived under governments that respected equal justice for all.)

Now, twenty-five years after the overthrow of Reconstruction, blacks had been widely disfranchised and forced back into semi-servitude. Without trial, mobs murdered blacks by hanging, shooting, burning, and beating. Such lynchings were a daily tragedy. Over 1,500 African-Americans were lynched during the 1890s. In 1900 there were another 115 lynchings; in 1901, another 130. It has become a *habit*, said Mark Twain. And in almost all of these cases, the killers went free.

Why did TR invite Washington to the White House? TR's chief aim in his first term was to be nominated and elected in 1904. He wanted to discuss with Washington what federal jobs should be handed out to southern blacks and whites, patronage to strengthen TR's support in the next election. He was acting not on any principle of racial equality but for political advantage.

The Tuskegee leader's aim was to have jobs taken away from Populists, who had exploited racial prejudice, and given to less wild-eyed whites and to black Republicans. Advised by Washington, TR tried to appoint those whites who appeared willing to share control of the party with blacks. But he appointed fewer African-Americans to federal positions than any of his predecessors.

At the turn of the century, mob violence against African-Americans, known as "lynchings," was quite common, and these crimes mostly went unpunished.

His southern appointments, TR liked to believe, were entirely altruistic. He found it hard to admit that the major result of his patronage policy was to gain tighter control of the Republican party. His response to the outcry over the incident was to declare he would have Mr. Washington "to dine just as often as I please." But he quietly gave in. Never again would he ask an African-American to sit at the table with him.

Sometimes TR pleased African-Americans by his actions; sometimes he angered them. They approved of his invitation to Booker T. Washington, his closing of a Mississippi post office rather than giving in to white demands that he fire the black postmistress there, and his insistence on appointing an African-American as collector of the port of Charleston, despite powerful southern opposition.

At the same time TR spoke favorably of the old southern traditions and falsely asserted that most lynchings were the result of sexual assaults by black men upon white women. Earlier, in the 1890s, when a mob had lynched Italian workers in New Orleans, TR had written to his sister that he thought the lynchings were "rather a good thing."

Elected in his own right in 1904, TR felt he no longer needed to worry about the support of black voters. In speeches given in 1905, he praised white racial purity and called the African-Americans a "backward race." Then, in August 1906, came an event that revealed how deeply ingrained was TR's racism. Earlier that month three companies of the Twenty-fifth Infantry—African-American units—were transferred to a fort on the Rio Grande just outside Brownsville, Texas. The local white people resented their presence, and several incidents occurred between them and the black soldiers. On the night of August 13, some people, never identified, fired guns in the town, and one white man was killed.

An army investigator was sent in. He concluded that some of the black troops must be guilty, although he could not name a single one. He added that the other black soldiers surely knew who the guilty ones were and he insisted that they had a duty to name the guilty men. In the three companies were men with records of fifteen and twenty-five years of military service. Six of them had been awarded the Congressional Medal of Honor.

Probably because he feared the effect on the black vote in the congressional elections, TR waited until the day afterward, November 5, to order that everyone in the three companies be discharged without honor and be forever barred from federal employment in either a military or a civilian capacity. Yet two weeks later he wrote a friend that he would "not for one moment consider the political effect" of his decision.

Booker T. Washington, notified in advance of the president's intention, tried to talk him out of making what he felt

★

to be a bad mistake. When the decision was announced, the African-Americans, said a black editor, felt "their alienation from the President, once their idol has been spontaneous, bitter, and universal." Some newspapers compared Brownsville with the Dreyfus Affair, in which Alfred Dreyfus, a Jewish army officer, had been framed for treason by anti-Semites in the military. They declared that racial prejudice in the American military was as pervasive as anti-Semitism in the French forces.

In 1970 after extensive research into documentary evidence, John D. Weaver published a book, *The Brownsville Raid,* that promoted congressional action to rectify TR's racist decision. The book reveals that the president went to great lengths to establish the guilt of the soldiers, not *before,* but *after* he had ordered their dismissal. He even used private investigators, paying government money, to extract false confessions from some of the soldiers and to collect dubious evidence of their involvement.

As a result of Weaver's work, African-American congressmen pressed for the soldiers' cause. In 1972 honorable discharges were recorded for the 167 infantrymen. One soldier, aged eighty-six, accepted formal restitution for his dead comrades. Weaver's book strongly suggests that the soldiers were framed by citizens of Brownsville.

It's worth noting that TR's autobiography does not mention Booker T. Washington. Nor is there any reference to Brownsville. Perhaps he preferred to forget his role in what the New York *World* called an "executive lynching."

Nor is there any reference to Atlanta. Only a month after Brownsville, on a September Saturday in 1906, when Atlanta was full of rural people, a mob of ten thousand white people, most of them under twenty, chased blacks through the streets, beating and killing them, and putting the torch to the property of African-Americans. They were aided and abetted by officers of the law, who gave no protection to blacks. "Atlanta brought shame to the South," wrote the Memphis *Commercial Appeal.* But from the Roosevelt White House came only silence.

16

MUCKRAKERS AND PROGRESSIVES

By the time the nominating conventions came around in 1904, victory looked like a sure thing for TR. He was unanimously chosen by the Republicans, with Charles W. Fairbanks of Indiana as his running mate. The party platform, as most do, fudged the issues and proclaimed that the Republicans were the true guardians of prosperity, while the Democrats would plunge the nation into disaster. The Democrats, remembering their losses when Bryan headed their ticket, turned conservative too. Their candidate was Alton B. Parker, chief judge of the New York State courts, with Henry G. Davis of West Virginia for vice president.

The campaign was dull. Both presidential candidates stayed close to home. In October it ignited briefly when the New York *World* demanded to know why TR's Bureau of Corporations, in existence 583 days, had done nothing. Was it because the corporations had poured big sums into his party's campaign treasury? The public ought to know how much had been given by the trusts, and the paper named them: beef, paper, coal, sugar, oil, tobacco, steel, banking, insurance.

To which TR responded cleverly. He did not deny that the corporations had given large sums. (They had, and the public had no way of knowing how much. In those days no law required campaign managers to report on contributions. And customarily, all financial records were burned.) But TR said it was false to claim that such contributions had been given as blackmail in return for silence regarding damaging facts gathered by the Bureau of Corporations.

TR on the campaign trail during the 1904 presidential race

The denial got national play in the press. TR was elected overwhelmingly. He had 336 electoral votes to 140 for Parker, and a popular majority of over 2,500,000. Ecstatic over his victory, TR made a pledge he would regret years later. He said that in view of "the wise custom which limits the President to two terms . . . under no circumstances will I be a candidate for or accept another nomination."

Elected to the presidency in his own right, the cocky TR felt now he could do as he wished. In his next message to Congress he stressed the need for federal action to correct corporate abuses, to provide workmen's compensation laws, to eliminate child labor abuses, and to end bribery and corruption in federal elections. It scared the industrialists who had poured all that money into his campaign. Soon afterward, he made a speech in Philadelphia that alarmed them even more.

He said: "The great development of industrialism means that there must be an increase in the supervision exercised by the Government over business enterprise. . . . Neither this people nor any other free people will permanently tolerate the use of the vast power conferred by vast wealth without lodging somewhere in the Government the still higher power of seeing that this power is used for and not against the interests of the people as a whole."

While TR thought big business needed to be curbed, he never wanted a new economic order to replace the old. He was deeply conservative on that question. If the industrialists and financiers were too self-satisfied, too smug, too stupid to avoid making serious mistakes and to correct them, he must step into the picture. He wanted to preserve the old order— if necessary, from the very people who profited most by it.

But investigative journalists during his early years in the White House began to publish article after article, book after book, with exposures of what was glaringly wrong with both business and politics, and this upset TR. He worried much about the rise of radicalism, and about the growing popularity of militant reformers. He charged some of the writers were "Socialists . . . merely lurid sensationalists . . . building up a revolutionary feeling." In a speech in 1906, he said they were like the man with the muckrake in John Bunyan's *Pilgrim's Progress* who was so busy raking the dirt that he never looked up or tried to do anything about it. But TR did not slow down the journalists. They took his word "muckraking" as a badge of honor. It was proof that their work was hitting home.

Lincoln Steffens, a young California journalist, is perhaps the best example of the muckrakers. As an editor of *McClure's* magazine, he helped launch the writing of detailed and careful studies of the corruption of governments—city and state— and of the corporations. His articles on eight American cities, collected in the 1904 book, *The Shame of the Cities,* caused a national sensation. *McClure's* also published Ida Tarbell's series exposing Standard Oil's ruthless ways, and Ray Stannard Baker's series depicting the grim conditions of African-American life.

In 1904 Robert Hunter, a young settlement-house worker,

★

Teddy Roosevelt denounced the new breed of reporter-reformers as "muckrakers," but these journalists saw his angry reaction as a measure of their own success.

Lincoln Steffens and Ida Tarbell, two of America's leading investigative journalists during TR's presidency

shocked the country with *Poverty*, a portrait of the ten million Americans living below the poverty line of $460 a year for a family of five. Reaching into the top levels of government, David Graham Phillips in *The Treason of the Senate* (1906), showed how politics and business connived in legislation.

Realistic fiction, too, did its part in muckraking. Frank Norris, in *The Octopus* (1901), dramatized the railroads' stranglehold on the farmers. And in 1906 came *The Jungle*, by Upton Sinclair, a young writer who had spent two years investigating the conditions in the Chicago stockyards. In his story of a family of Lithuanian immigrants, he worked in the revolting details of how meat was contaminated, how spoiled hams were treated with formaldehyde, how sausages were made from rotten meat scraps, rats, and other garbage. His bestseller caused a national outcry for better regulation of the meat-packing industry.

TR, despite his attack upon muckrakers, listened. He, too, was so disgusted that he gave up his favorite breakfast sausage. He ordered an inquiry into the industry's conditions and used the report to pressure Congress and the packers to accept a reform bill. The Meat Inspection Act of 1906 was a compromise, meeting some demands for better inspection and sanitary standards but giving in to the packers on other issues. Many progressives were unhappy with the outcome, but TR would always settle for half a loaf rather than none.

On the same day in 1906 as the meat bill passed, Congress passed another important law, the Pure Food and Drug Act. It was pushed by reformers, writers, and government officials who took advantage of the hullabaloo raised by *The Jungle's* exposé. They had called for a law to regulate the sale of food and drugs, especially the huge number of patented medicines sold through the mail, by traveling salesmen, and in local stores. Wildly extravagant claims were made for these products, and many package and canned foods contained alcohol and dangerous impurities—even such narcotics as cocaine and opium. The effect was to make addicts of many consumers, including women and children.

The success of the muckrakers was partly due to a revolution in journalism that had begun in the 1890s. New magazines like *McClure's*, with slick formats and advertising, were selling far better than the older elite periodicals such as *Scribner's* and *Harper's*. The new publications appealed to a broad public whose conscience had been awakened by the mounting class conflicts.

A dozen other magazines joined *McClure's* in printing fact-packed articles of exposure—*Collier's*, *Hampton's*, the *American*, *Cosmopolitan*, *Munsey's*, the *Arena*, *Everybody's*. . . . Almost every mass-circulation magazine followed the trend. The writers burrowed into every major industry, into every cog and wheel of the political machinery, into the universities, the churches, the courts, the Senate, the government agencies, even the women's clubs.

Contrary to TR's fears, the muckrakers were never revolutionary. They were simply reformers, voicing anger at corruption that reduced opportunity, and calling for moderate changes to remedy the situation. As one of them said, "We are going to expose evil in order to replace it by good."

The muckrakers rose out of what has been called the Progressive movement. Progressives hoped to persuade people to become active, well-informed citizens. They were optimists who believed social changes could be made and that government should take an active role in investigating and correcting abuses brought on by economic or technological change. They hoped to move the country toward social justice. The writings of the muckrakers did much to infuse the Progressive movement with enthusiasm and righteousness. The corruption and centralized power they attacked did exist. But they were symptoms, not causes. TR's vivid expression of progressive themes shaped the public image of him as a fighter for reform, and it gave strength to the movement. But he had no real program for dealing with big business. He blustered about trust-busting, yet was never eager to dig out wrongdoing by the big corporations. He believed that private property was vital to both society and the individual. His long-range view was to preserve

★

the property system by getting the people who ran it to act more humanely and the economy to run more efficiently. That was how the Progressive movement itself, made up mostly of middle-class reformers, felt.

Did such attitudes bring results? Yes, in some ways and to some degree, as we have seen. But basically the Progressive crusade ended in indifference or disillusionment. The reformers found the system had a tremendous inertia that resisted change. Tinkering with administrative methods or political procedures might produce a minor difference here or there. But nothing cut into the power structure of the corporate system.

Nor is it surprising that the Progressives moved within narrow limits. A well-educated, middle-class group, they were economically secure, and their reforms came more from the head rather than from the gut. Like TR, they were ambitious for personal power. They looked to "the strong man" for political leadership, the man dedicated to the social good. Few thought of themselves as servants of the people. Rather, their role in government was to "give justice from above," as TR often said. The mass of society needed such "benevolent guardians" as themselves.

Typical of them, as well as of TR, was their attitude toward the great influx of immigrants during this period—the people from southern and eastern Europe and Asia. They called them "indigestible aliens," "undesirables," and "inferior races," who would pollute the "clean Aryan blood." Still, while many Progressives were anti-immigrant, anti-Catholic, and anti-Jewish, they tried to live by the Christian ethic and the democratic tradition. They were not ruthless like the Ku Klux Klansmen, or like the Nazis who would one day devastate Europe. TR appointed Jews and Catholics to his cabinet, and pressured California to live up to the Constitution in its treatment of Asian Americans.

The middle class, including the Progressives, were as upset by the rise of labor unions as by the rise of the trusts. They feared such collective action from below by working people even more than the collective action from above by the corporations. Nevertheless, in those early years of the twentieth century, many gains were made for labor, chiefly at the state level. New state laws limited the workday, tens of thousands of working people won the eight-hour day through their unions, many states set age limits and restricted hours for child labor, and workmen's compensation laws provided payments for employees injured in industrial accidents.

17

THE CONSERVATIONIST

On the domestic front nothing he accomplished gratified TR more than what he did for conservation. When he entered the White House he extended nationally the conservation program he had started for New York State. He knew that half of America's forests had been destroyed, the rivers polluted and filled with silt, the land eroded, and many species of animals placed on the verge of extinction.

The nation was lucky to have TR reach the presidency at this moment. No one was so well prepared to carry out a badly needed conservation program. His instinctive love of nature (we saw it expressed in his childhood), and his training and practical experience, made him alive to the urgent necessity to take political action on this issue. His years as a state legislator, a governor, and a federal official had taught him how to maneuver the passage of constructive legislation. Now, with the highest power in his hands, he carried out a comprehensive, nationwide conservation program.

TR's interest in conservation began long before he became New York's governor. During his early hunting days out west, he had sensed the dangers threatening the large game animals in that part of the country. To protect them from wholesale slaughter he had formed in 1887 a group of wealthy sportsmen called the Boone and Crockett Club, named for two of TR's heroes. Electing TR the club's president, the members centered on the preservation of large game. Soon the club's energies turned also to forest and land conservation. Several of

President Roosevelt, with naturalist John Muir at his left, at the base of a giant sequoia in Yosemite National Park

the nation's leading legislators and scientists joined the club, adding greatly to its influence on public opinion and Congress.

The Boone and Crockett was by no means the only sportsmen's club committed to the perpetuation of wildlife and their habitats. Hundreds of clubs of fishermen and hunters had begun to form in the 1870s, and they played an increasing role in the conservation movement. TR, a Harvard student then, would not turn his mind to conservation until his western expeditions began.

One of the first achievements of the sports clubs was to get Congress to pass in 1894 the Park Protection Act, which saved Yellowstone National Park, created in 1872, from becoming a commercial disaster. It became illegal to kill the birds, mammals, and other animals in Yellowstone, thus establishing the country's first federal wildlife sanctuary. The clubs also pushed through, in 1891, the Forest Reserve Act, which laid the foundation for the present national forest reserve system.

Just before President McKinley's death, the Nevada Senator Francis G. Newlands had introduced a bill in Congress authorizing the federal government to build irrigation projects in sixteen western states, which was to be financed by the sale of public lands. The reclaimed land was then to be sold to settlers, with the proceeds going to additional projects. The bill might have died in Congress if TR had not seized upon it as soon as he became president. He managed to get it adopted in 1902, and the Reclamation Act opened the way for construction of dams whose impounded water would irrigate arid lands previously incapable of growing crops. Later he called for extending irrigation projects to the South Atlantic and Gulf States, to reclaim swampland.

Following through on this, he launched a massive educational program to inform the public of the needs and purposes of practical forestry. He knew this was vital to protect the program from attacks by commercial interests that were concerned only with exploiting the timberlands for the greatest and quickest profits. He said again and again that the forests were not there for the present generation alone. They were "for the people," and these words "must always include the people unborn as well as the people now alive, or the democratic ideal is not realized."

TR tried to rouse the public to the importance of the forests in soil and water conservation. If the wholesale cutting of trees continued, it would increase the likelihood of erosion and floods. In his last annual message to Congress he used photographs—the first time any president had done this—to make the legislators see the destructive effect in China of the devastation of the forests in its northern mountain region. And then he explained its impact:

> The lesson of deforestation in China is a lesson which mankind should have learned many times already from what has occurred in other places. Denudation leaves naked soil; then gullying cuts down to the bare rock; and meanwhile the rock-waste buries the bottomlands. When the soil is gone, men must go, and the process does not take long. . . . What has happened in central Asia, in Palestine, in north Africa, in parts of the Mediterranean countries of Europe, will surely happen in our country if we do not exercise that wise foresight which should be one of the chief marks of any people calling itself civilized.

While working to preserve the forests, TR made use of the authority that presidents had to set aside forest reserves from the public domain. During his two terms, he added nearly 150 million acres of forestland to the reserves. This tripled the acreage set aside by all earlier presidents.

Toward the end of his time in the White House, TR became worried about the failure thus far to create national forests in the eastern United States. He wanted the forests of the White Mountains and the southern Appalachians to be preserved, too. In a 1907 speech on Arbor Day, he spoke eloquently about the future of the nation's trees:

★

*President Roosevelt with Chief Forester Gifford Pinchot
on the deck of a river steamer during a 1907 trip of the
newly established Internal Waterways Commission*

We of the older generation can get along with what we have, though with growing hardship, but in your full manhood and womanhood you will want what nature once so beautifully supplied and man so thoughtlessly destroyed; and because of that want you will reproach us, not for what we have used, but for what we have wasted. . . . So any nation which in its youth lives only for the day, reaps without sowing, and consumes without husbanding, must expect the penalty of the prodigal whose labor could with difficulty find him the bare means of life.

It took a while, after the Yellowstone wildlife sanctuary was established, for people to see that wildlife everywhere needed protection of this kind. Hadn't hunters reduced the millions of buffalo to less than one thousand? And what about the passenger pigeon? Once numbering in the billions, blotting out the sun when they flew across the skies, weren't they now wiped out to the point where no one believed rumors of the sighting of a single one? The same fate threatened still other animals when TR took office.

His first move to protect wildlife came when ornithologists appealed to him to save the birds of Pelican Island, a tiny spot of land in Florida's Indian River. Here hunters of bird feathers to decorate women's hats had almost extinguished the egrets, ibises, roseate spoonbills, and other colorful birds. By executive order TR declared Pelican Island a federal bird sanctuary. It was the country's first federal wildlife refuge. From this small beginning he would go on to create four additional refuges in many parts of the continental United States, as well as in Puerto Rico, Alaska, and Hawaii.

Of course, he did not act alone; he was joined in the movement by individual crusaders as well as many organizations, such as the National Audubon Society and the U.S. Biological Survey. But if not for TR's presence in the White House, who knows how long it might have taken to achieve such great conservation measures?

★

TR with naturalist and author John Burroughs during
a visit to the Yellowstone National Park in 1903

When TR became president, there were only five national
parks: Yosemite, Yellowstone, Sequoia, Mount Rainier, and
General Grant. Congress added five more under his pressure.
And today the nation can take pride in counting some forty
national parks. Every year many millions of people visit them
to enjoy their grandeur and their beauty.

TR broadened the meaning of conservation, to include
minerals and oil reserves as well as power sites. "The mineral
wealth of the country," he said, "the coal, iron, oil, gas, and
the like, does not reproduce itself and therefore is certain
to be exhausted ultimately." In 1908 he called a National
Conservation Congress to consider every aspect of conserva-

tion. All the state governors attended, the Supreme Court justices, congresspeople, scientists, experts on the nation's natural resources, and foreign diplomats. TR opened the congress, urging that government power be more widely used for the purpose of conservation, not only at the national level but at the state and municipal levels as well.

The conference brought about quick action. The state governors endorsed its proposals, and most of them set up state conservation commissions. Scientific organizations appointed similar committees, and a National Conservation Commission was established. TR's initiative gave the movement the prestige and momentum that it needed to enable it to surmount the occasional political reversals it would encounter during future administrations.

Not that all was smooth sailing during TR's own administration. He often tangled with Congress over policy on natural resources. Power companies, lumbermen, mine operators, and ranchers lobbied against him, believing that they had a sacred right to exploit the country's resources. They hated any attempt to limit their operations. But TR usually prevailed, swinging the voters behind him through fervent moral appeals, and the Congress through clever political tactics.

Within a year of the 1908 Congress, the National Conservation Commission completed the task of making an inventory of the nation's natural resources—the first such listing any country had ever attempted. And early in 1909, shortly before TR's term as president ended, he brought together in the White House representatives of Canada and Mexico for the first North American Conservation Conference. He hoped for still another conference, to include representatives from dozens of nations who would combine efforts for an international conservation program. But his successor, President Taft, did not follow up on it. Not for another fifty years would international conferences on such a scale be held.

There is little question that one of TR's most important contributions as president was his vision of conservation.

18

THE BIG STICK

Domestic policy and foreign policy—these are the two sides of a president's responsibilities. Some presidents pay far more attention to the one than to the other. In part it depends on their personal leanings. TR was the kind of president who played a big role in domestic affairs and just as big a role in foreign policy. Surely his own nature—his boundless energy, his pleasure in taking charge, in using his executive powers to the limit and sometimes beyond—had a lot to do with his readiness to act on all fronts.

When he entered the White House the world was jittery with rivalry and tension. The United States, Germany, and Japan had risen rapidly in industrial strength and were challenging Great Britain's dominance. They were building fleets to carry their power to foreign shores. Each nation wanted to carve out a global empire for itself. By 1901, as TR took office, many of the weaker nations had been grabbed up by the older imperial powers—Britain, France, Russia. By the time America joined the international competition, almost all of Africa and most of Asia had been carved into colonies. So the newcomers had to compete among themselves and against the older powers in building empires.

TR saw the international competition for an empire as dependent basically on force. He defined his approach in strong terms: "I have always been fond," he said, "of the West African proverb 'Speak softly and carry a big stick; you will go far.' " But he liked to believe that there was more to success than superior brute force—we were a civilized power, we stood for enlightenment and culture, we were the protectors of law and order, the defenders of freedom, the carriers of justice and democracy.

In his first message to Congress. TR noted that wars between the "civilized" powers were no longer as common as they had once been. But conflict between these superior nations and what he called the "semi-barbarian peoples" was frequent. Yet this did not seem to trouble him, for such warfare was "merely a most regrettable but necessary police duty, which must be performed for the sake of the welfare of mankind."

Sure that progress was inevitable and that America's role was to spread civilization (its version of it) everywhere possible, TR shaped an energetic and ambitious foreign policy. While he talked in ethical and cultural terms of this civilizing mission, businessmen scoured the world looking for additional markets for American products. Their interests—the empire newly won from Spain—had to be protected. That meant ensuring control of the Caribbean and the cutting of a canal through the isthmus of Central America so that naval power could be easily transferred from one ocean to the other.

The history of the canal goes back to a time long before TR became president. But it isn't necessary to go through the complicated diplomatic maneuvers and intrigues in Europe and Latin America that finally placed the canal project under U.S. control. In 1902 Congress approved a canal route through Panama (then a part of Colombia) instead of Nicaragua. The next year a pact was made with Colombia that granted the United States the right to construct the canal. But the Colombian Congress rejected the pact, even though the United States threatened Colombia would regret it if she did not ratify the pact without modifying any of its provisions. The Colombians felt it was a poor deal that offered their country only trifling compensation and that seriously cut into its sovereignty.

*Seizing on the appearance of a U.S. warship off Panama,
the cartoonist used it to symbolize TR's "Big Stick" policy,
designed to get his way in foreign affairs.*

Result? Angry at not having his own way with those "contemptible little creatures," TR told several important friends that it would be convenient if Panama were an independent state. But he didn't say that publicly, "lest it be taken as an effort to incite insurrection in Panama." Soon newspapers were printing stories about impending revolution in Panama. And on November 3, 1903, the predicted uprising broke out. It was financed and inspired by a small group of men in New York. Their money bought some five hundred mercenaries, who were joined by about the same number of men from

*TR poses at the controls of a giant steam shovel during work
on the San Miguel lock of the Panama Canal in 1906.*

Panama's fire department. The same day, a U.S. warship, with neat timing, suddenly appeared on the scene to prevent Colombia from putting down the revolt. TR's secretary of state, Elihu Root, warned that the United States would block any effort by Colombia to restore authority over the area. An hour after getting news of the revolt, TR recognized the new government. And two weeks later Panama and the United States signed a treaty granting the United States the desired canal rights. By 1914, five years after TR had left the White House, the gigantic construction project was completed, and the canal opened for traffic. TR would always be touchy about the charge that he acted in a lawless and unethical manner. Yet he could not resist boasting publicly, "I took the Canal Zone." The Panama affair, as historian George Mowry wrote, suggests that for TR "ethics stopped at the tidewater beyond which lay a moral jungle where power was the only rightful determinant."

With naval bases established in the Caribbean and with greater political control of the surrounding countries secure, the Caribbean became, in effect, a dependency of the United States, "an American lake," as some put it. In the years to come, the United States would be quick to use force (the marines) to guarantee that no basic decisions contrary to U.S. interests would be tolerated.

What happened in Cuba is but one example. After the Spanish-American War, Cuba was, in form at least, an independent nation. In fact, however, Cuba became a satellite of the United States. In March 1901, the Platt Amendment to an army appropriations bill guaranteed that. Under Platt, Cuba could not permit a foreign power to secure even partial control and could not incur any debts that might bring about foreign intervention. The United States could step in to preserve order and maintain Cuban independence, and Cuba would sell or lease naval bases to the United States. Under pressure, the Cubans worked the Platt Amendment into their constitution in June 1901. They had little choice; either you do it, the United States said, or we won't withdraw our troops from the island. In 1903, a treaty between the two nations cemented the agreement so that the Cubans could not kill it by constitutional amendment.

Then TR proclaimed the "Roosevelt Corollary" to the Monroe Doctrine. The Monroe Doctrine had been fashioned against the ambitions of Europe. The corollary reshaped it against the sovereignty of Latin America. From now on, TR said in 1904, when nations of the Western Hemisphere do anything that might encourage European intervention, the United States will step in to forestall such action. Naturally, this policy pleased American corporations. It secured their access to markets without interference. In the next dozen years their exports to Latin America more than doubled. TR carried out this policy not only in Cuba but in several other countries of the Caribbean and Latin America. "Dollar Diplomacy," people would soon call it. Other administrations since TR's have followed pretty much the same policy in that region.

Something similar happened far from Cuba, on the other side of the world. As a result of the treaty ending the war with Spain, Spain ceded to the United States the countries of Puerto Rico, Guam, and the Philippines. Less than 400 miles from the coast of China the 7,100 islands of the Philippines were considered strategically vital to American expansion.

Public opinion split sharply over what to do about the Philippines. The easy victory over Spain had raised the American flag up over the islands, and once it goes up, said TR's friend Senator Lodge, "It must never come down." But many prominent Americans rejected the adoption of an imperial policy. Scores of thousands joined the American Anti-Imperialist League. Among its endorsers were two former presidents, Benjamin Harrison and Grover Cleveland. The league's aim was to oppose, "by every legitimate means, the acquisition of the Philippine Islands or any colonies away from our shores." The league platform called the "subjugation" of the Philippines "criminal aggression" and "betrayal" of the basic principles of the Declaration of Independence and the Constitution.

But the man who had the greatest influence on the American decision did not see it that way. President McKinley had

★

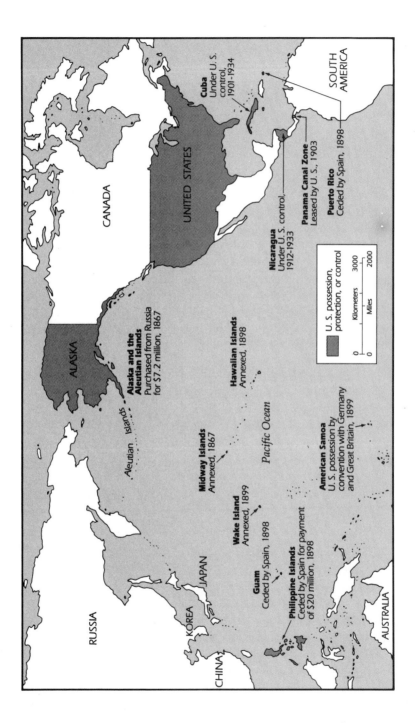

concluded that we must keep the Philippines. Why? Because, as he would say later, the islands were a base en route to China, with its 400 million potential customers.

It was a turning point for the American future. Up to that time, except for Alaska, the United States had always granted self-rule in areas that it had acquired. But another of TR's friends, Senator Albert Beveridge, in a passionate speech ridiculed the notion "that we ought not to govern a people without their consent." He said: "The rule of liberty that all just government derives its authority from the consent of the governed applies only to those who are capable of self-government. We govern the Indians without their consent, we govern our territories without their consent, we govern our children without their consent."

And why not the Philippines? he asked.

Because, said the people of the islands, we want to govern ourselves. The "backward" Filipinos showed little enthusiasm for a "civilizing" process that robbed them of independence. To make the Philippines a colony, the United States had to suppress the revolution of its people. Earlier, in 1898, under their leader, Emilio Aguinaldo, the Filipinos had risen up against the Spanish and proclaimed their independence. They believed that the United States would grant freedom and independence to them. But when the treaty with Spain gave the United States control of the Philippines, the Filipinos had launched an armed revolt against U.S. rule. To suppress the uprising, the United States sent in 70,000 troops, adding more and more men as resistance continued.

Atrocities against the Filipinos were common. The American general "Hell-Roaring" Jake Smith, issued oral orders: "I want no prisoners. I wish you to kill and burn; the more you kill and burn, the better you will please me." In a letter home, one army officer wrote, "Our men have been relentless, have killed to exterminate men, women and children, prisoners and captives, active insurgents and suspected people, from lads of ten up, an idea prevailing that the Filipino was little better than a dog."

The army set up concentration camps to isolate the population from the revolutionaries, for clearly, said a War Department report, behind the guerrillas is "almost complete unity of action of the entire population." Anyone seen outside the camp zones was considered an enemy and shot on sight. The crops decayed in the fields, and deserted homes fell apart. The number who died in those camps, and outside them, is unknown. But the *New York Times* reported that one-sixth of Luzon's population of about 600,000 was exterminated on that island alone. Torture methods such as the "water cure" and the "rope treatment" were used to make prisoners talk, or die. Recognizing the horrors of America's actions in the Philippines, writer Mark Twain suggested that the American flag should have "the white stripes painted black and the stars replaced by the skull and crossbones."

As for TR's view, he told a German diplomat, "I have taken care that the army should understand that I thoroughly believe in severe methods when necessary, and am not in the least sensitive about killing any number of men if there is adequate reason. But I do not like torture or needless brutality."

Upon a report that General J. Franklin Bell's scorched-earth campaign had killed one-third of the population of Batangas Province in southern Luzon, through shooting, starvation, and war-induced disease, TR sent the general a letter of congratulations.

While the American troops were devastating the Filipino countryside, negotiations went on, in an attempt to appease Filipino nationalists with the promise of limited concessions. Businessmen worried that Spanish and English corporations were the only ones active in the islands; they wanted a peace that would clear the way for American capital to make investments.

On July 4, 1902, TR prematurely declared the war over, and Congress passed the Philippine Organic Act, promising independence. But it took another half century for independence to be granted. Meanwhile, resistance by guerrilla bands continued sporadically until 1911, when their last leader was captured and executed. This was no "splendid little war," like that of 1898. Over 125,000 U.S. soldiers fought, and over 4,000 died in the islands. About five times that many Filipinos were killed in combat, and to that number must be added another 250,000 civilian deaths due to the fighting, malnutrition, and disease.

TR delighted in foreign affairs, where a president had much more freedom of action than in domestic matters. He liked to operate alone, dealing with other nations, without day-to-day haggling with the Congress. Generally he acted as his own secretary of state, sometimes even bypassing his cabinet and members of the foreign service. He showed disrespect, even disdain, for what the Congress and the public thought about foreign policy. That attitude set a precedent other presidents have followed.

TR's biggest trophy in foreign policy was the Nobel Peace Prize (1906), awarded for his work as mediator in settling the Russo-Japanese War of 1904–1905 at the peace conference in Portsmouth, New Hampshire. Ever the strong executive, he prided himself on his use of power. "The biggest matters," he said, "such as the Portsmouth Peace, the acquisition of Panama, and sending the fleet around the world, I managed without consultation with anyone; for when a matter is of capital importance, it is well to have it handled by one man only."

Periodically TR and his successors in the White House would send marines into the Caribbean and Latin America to protect American investments. Always the language that they used to justify such actions was high-flown, brushing over the hard material interests that lay beneath. "America's duty toward the people living in barbarism," TR said, "is to see that they are freed from their chains and we can free them only by destroying barbarism itself." In his own mind he divided the world into "civilized" and "barbarous" nations. So did many others in those days.

TR made many excursions into foreign affairs beyond those already discussed. In dealing with major powers such as Great

Britain, France, Germany, and China, he acted one way. And in dealing with the "Dagoes" of Latin America, quite another way. Those whom the United States towered over he would refer to as "jackrabbits," "foolish and contemptible corruptionists," or "inefficient bandits." If these weaker nations made difficulties, he would get so angry that he did not hesitate to distort the facts. When convinced he was morally right (and when was he not?), he could assert that what *he* wanted to do was "therefore justified in law."

19

THE BULL MOOSE
CHARGES AGAIN

When TR's forty-sixth birthday came around on October 27, 1904, his friend and secretary of state, Elihu Root, sent him a playful note of congratulations. "You have made a very good start in life," he wrote, "and your friends have great hopes for you when you grow up."

Four years later, TR had just turned fifty when his presidency ended. It is a sad thing for presidents when they leave office at so young an age. What are they to do with the rest of their lives? Politics was TR's greatest love; he had held the highest office any politician could aspire to. Yet precedent dictated that he quit now, and exit gracefully.

As his last term wound down, he worried over his future. To enter the world of business would be distasteful. What about the presidency of Harvard? The position had just become available. TR was a Harvard man, a scholar, an author, and a proven executive. But the post was not offered to him. Then why not follow President John Quincy Adams, who had served honorably and courageously in Congress for many years after leaving the White House? TR liked the idea of running for the Senate, but nothing came of it. By the fall of 1908 he had made his decision. He would use his talents to write a dozen articles a year for the *Outlook,* a weekly journal whose editorial position agreed with his, and the magazine could pay him well.

Meanwhile, there was the question of who would succeed him. Presidents usually try to have much to say about that. In 1908 TR brought about the nomination of William Howard

Taft, his secretary of war. Taft, an Ohio lawyer, had been a federal judge, dean of a law school, U.S. solicitor general, and the civil governor of the Philippines. TR believed he would continue his programs. Then rumors spread that TR meant to retract his pledge of 1904 that he would not run again. If that had been true, his popularity was still so great that he would easily have been reelected. Instead, TR used his considerable influence to ensure that Taft would be nominated at the Republican convention. Meanwhile, the Democrats trotted out the hopeless Bryan for his third and last try at the presidency. Taft was elected, but by only half the popular majority by which TR had won in 1904.

With Taft safely in the White House, TR was ready for a one-year hunting trip in Africa. As he left the presidency there was a whirlwind of partisan comment; no wonder, for everything he did always raised nearly as many jeers as cheers. The loftiest praise came from Taft, who declared that historians would "accord Roosevelt a place with Washington and Lincoln." At the other extreme was the newspaper editor who called TR "a perpetual self-seeker . . . a foxy twister of the facts . . . a daringly pernicious and noisy politician." Some papers knocked TR by praising Taft: "There will now be a reign of reason in the White House." The New York *Sun*, which had always detested TR, printed only one word on its editorial page on the day he left the White House: "Thru!" Even after returning to private life, for the first time since his early twenties, TR would remain in the glare of the spotlight. "He is his own limelight and could not help it," wrote his friend the novelist Owen Wister. "A creature charged with such voltage as his became the central presence at once, whether he stepped on a platform or entered a room."

True, the vitality was there, at least on the surface. But underneath? TR was blind in one eye and saw poorly with the other. He was much overweight, and he still suffered from a recurrent fever he had picked up in Cuba. And there was that leg injury from which he never had recovered. Still, he ignored all this; he was sure no harm could come to him in Africa.

TR's first impulse had been to make the African trip with

*Teddy Roosevelt, with his son Kermit, displaying
trophies from their African hunting expedition in 1909*

only his son Kermit, now twenty. Not a wealthy man, TR
financed his trip by signing a contract with *Scribner's* magazine
for $50,000 to write about his experiences. Then he persuaded
the Smithsonian Institution to send along three professional
field naturalists and taxonomists to prepare and ship back the
specimens they would collect. The scientists had heard TR
was a hard man to get along with, but they quickly found that
not to be true. They shared everything alike, and TR's "chief
thought," said one, "was for the welfare of the party." Another
scientist said that TR "demonstrated what a marvellous faunal
naturalist he was by acquiring a great mass of new observations
on the life histories of the animals with which we met."

★

At home the public followed TR's travels through dispatches to the American press from such exotic places as Mombasa, Nairobi, Uganda, Gondokoro. His adventures were devoured as avidly as if he were the new Marco Polo. The record of the animals he and Kermit slaughtered was stunning: a total of 512, including 17 lions, 11 elephants, 2 rhinoceroses, 8 hippopotamuses, 9 giraffes, 47 gazelles, 29 zebras, 9 hyenas, and a miscellaneous log of other creatures, with such names as the bongo, the kudu, the dik-dik, the wildebeest, the aardwolf, the klipspringer . . . real animals that ended up stuffed for exhibit in the National Museum at Washington.

When the expedition completed its descent of the Nile, it came out at Khartoum. With his customary self-assurance, TR proceeded to speak his mind on the explosive political situation. "In an atmosphere tense with dissension between ruling English and fanatically anti-English Egyptians," said the journalist Mark Sullivan, "Roosevelt . . . told the English they must continue to rule Egypt, the Egyptians that they must be loyal to the English."

His tour of Europe was like a royal procession: kings and queens and emperors all welcomed him. He concluded that they were nice people but on the average not very smart. "I can't imagine a more appallingly dreary life for a man of ambition and power," he said.

Universities lined up to confer upon him honorary degrees—in Stockholm, Brussels, Berlin, Cambridge, Oxford. In London he gave a speech advising the British how to run their empire. It provoked a debate in Parliament and caused one newspaper to note, "Mr. Roosevelt should learn that he is not exempt from the customs of civilized nations."

While TR was in Europe, King Edward VII of England died, and TR was asked by President Taft to serve as special ambassador of the United States to the funeral. TR's ironic view of the exalted posturings of the largest assembly of crowned heads the world had yet seen made for amusing table talk long after. Never again would he wish to attend a royal funeral. "I felt," he said, "if I met another king I should bite him."

★

On June 18, 1910, TR returned to New York. Having been gone fifteen months, he received thunderous applause from the vast crowd at the Battery. In a brief speech he said he was "ready and eager" to "help solve problems." Did that mean that he would like to be president again?

No, he wanted only privacy, "to close up like a native oyster" at his house at Sagamore Hill. He enjoyed once again his hours with Edith, their walks in the woods, the sunsets across the Sound, the great log fires indoors, his books and pictures and horses and, of course, his children.

But public affairs pressed him hard. While abroad he had received two thousand invitations to make speeches on his return, and now the requests continued to pile up. Normally, the prospect of political action was irresistible, but his relationship to Taft tortured him. He had put the man in the White House and therefore felt obliged to support him.

Yet he was unhappy with Taft. While TR was abroad, Taft had written to say that he had tried to carry out TR's policies, "but my method of doing so has not worked smoothly. . . . I have had a hard time." One thing he did that angered TR was to remove Chief Forester Gifford Pinchot, TR's passionate supporter of conservation programs. Of greater importance was a revolt in the Congress by young progressive Republicans against the old-guard leadership. The insurgents won, but TR felt that Taft had handled the situation badly. In another fight over the tariff, Taft again mishandled the issue, as TR saw it. But the real cause of the trouble was a clash of personalities. TR and Taft simply didn't manage matters in the same way.

But if TR criticized Taft, it would be public admission that TR had made a bad mistake. Yet how could he remain silent? Wouldn't some say that meant he condoned what Taft did, while others would take silence as criticism? And then there was his commitment to write for the *Outlook*. How could he discuss public affairs and not mention the president?

Reluctantly, TR became involved in the 1910 elections. But how "reluctantly"? That summer and fall he made a long

★

speaking tour through the West and the South. Supposedly, it was to support Republican candidates. Actually, it focused public attention upon himself, not on them. In his speeches he began to outline elements of a political program that he called the New Nationalism, which moved him to the left, to a more progressive position than ever before. Attacking the Supreme Court's conservative attitude toward social legislation, he quoted Lincoln's statement that labor is "prior to and independent of capital" and deserved higher consideration. "I stand for the square deal," TR said, "but I mean not merely that I stand for fair play under the present rules of the game, but that I stand for having those rules changed so as to work for a more substantial equality of opportunity and reward."

He went even further when he said: "We are face to face with new conceptions of the relations of property to human welfare. The man who wrongly holds that every human right is secondary to his profit must now give way to the advocate of human welfare, who rightly maintains that every man holds his property subject to the general right of the community to regulate its use to whatever degree the public welfare may require it."

In his home state of New York, TR helped bring about the nomination of a friend for governor. But despite TR's endorsement, the man lost badly to a Democrat. It seemed the people were tired of the long Republican rule. And "a little tired of me," said TR. The House of Representatives went Democratic, too, while in New Jersey a presidential hopeful, Woodrow Wilson, won the governorship on the Democratic ticket. Now all this, said TR, "will put a stop to the talk about my being nominated in 1912, which was beginning to make me very uneasy."

TR was responding to a new wave of progressive Republicans entering the Congress. They had taken the liberal route in state and city affairs, often defying the local Republican machines. Men such as Senator Robert M. La Follette of Wisconsin and Representative George W. Norris of Nebraska resisted the rigid rule of the regular party leadership. They wanted their party to stop acting as the mere tool of big business.

The Republican Party began to split dramatically. The rebels, now calling themselves Progressives, got stronger and stronger. To this dynamic wing of the party, President Taft was no longer acceptable. The rebels gathered around Senator La Follette to form the Progressive Republican League, bent on denying Taft the Republican nomination in 1912. At its founding convention in 1911 the league declared that its chief object was "the promotion of popular government and progressive legislation." Its platform called for direct election of U.S. senators, direct primaries for the nomination of elective officers, direct election of delegates to national conventions, amendment of state constitutions to provide for the initiative, the referendum and recall, and a corrupt practices act.

These were all democratizing measures designed to loosen the grip of party machines and to make it easier for the popular will to be expressed. The direct election of senators became part of the U.S Constitution in 1913, and many of the other reforms were gradually adopted at federal, state, or local levels.

By the time the presidential race of 1912 drew close, Governor Wilson of New Jersey had made a record in office that appeared to be much like TR's New Nationalism, only Wilson called his reform program the "New Freedom." Meanwhile, the relationship between Taft and TR was dying, if not already dead. TR had shifted away from policies he once backed and became more progressive, while Taft had gradually turned more conservative. La Follette had expected to be the party's nominee for president, but TR decided to take the regular Republican nomination away from Taft. He failed to do so: the right-wing party machine was too strong and feared the Progressive ideas TR was now advocating. TR would probably have been the choice of the majority of the party's rank and file, if the machine had not silenced their voices. So he bolted the party. This though he had long prided himself on being a regular party man who would never desert the Republicans.

★

Wilson was nominated by the Democrats on a liberal platform. Then the Progressives held a convention at Chicago to write their platform, and they put TR at the head of the ticket. The "Bull Moosers," they were called, taken from TR's comment that he felt as fit as a bull moose. The platform was considered radical for its time: it promised such things as the vote for women, a ban on child labor, and the eight-hour workday. It denounced "the unholy alliance between corrupt business and corrupt politics." It called for a national system of social insurance, and it endorsed trade unions.

Several Progressives, such as Jane Addams, Lillian Wald, and Joel Spingarn, excited by the promise of TR's new party, carried to the convention a plank drafted by Dr. W. E. B. Du Bois, a well-known African-American writer and spokesman for social change. It read: "The Progressive Party recognizes that distinctions of race or class in the political life have no place in a democracy. . . . The party therefore demands for the American of Negro descent the repeal of unfair discriminatory laws and the right to vote on the same terms on which other citizens vote." But TR would have none of it, and the plank was ignored.

TR took to the road once more in his last try for the presidency. It was a wearisome routine this time, and an uphill struggle. He smelled defeat in the air. On the evening of October 14, as he was leaving his hotel in Milwaukee to deliver a speech, TR was shot in the right breast by a man named John Schrank. The crowd swarmed over the gunman and probably would have lynched him if TR had not waved them off. How badly hurt he was, no one could tell. When doctors demanded that he be rushed at once to a hospital, he refused and ordered his driver to take him to the hall. "I will make this speech or die," he said.

At the hall, doctors found that the bullet had passed through him. But he insisted on standing up on the platform to speak while the crowd sat in numbed horror. His voice was so low and halting that few could understand his words. In the hospital, after he finished the brief talk, it was found that the bullet had penetrated his right lung, the impact lessened by its first having passed through his overcoat, his eyeglass case, and the folded manuscript of his speech. The doctors announced that the wound was not serious.

The public felt sympathy for TR and admired his courage. He spoke once more, two weeks later, at Madison Square Garden in New York, to a crowd of 11,000. Again he sounded the principles of the Progressives. But the election proved it was impossible for such a new party to erupt out of the Republican party and knock over both old parties at once. In the end, Wilson was elected with more than 6 million votes to TR's 4 million, while Taft came in a poor third. The Democrats also won both houses of Congress.

★

20

A SAFARI, A WAR, AND DEATH

Nothing much came of the Progressive Party. Made up of a gaggle of conflicting groups, it fell apart soon after the defeat of 1912. Only a small minority of reformers had hoped to make the new party national and permanent. With the excitement of an election gone and Wilson's Congress enacting several planks of the Progressive platform, the party's flimsy structure crumbled. It would make a last effort in the 1914 elections and then disappear. But many of its basic beliefs still influence American life.

In the spring of 1913, TR decided to head an expedition to explore the jungles of South America. It was a perilous mission. Now fifty-five, he was in poor shape to risk the extreme hardships of a little-known wilderness. He secured the support of the American Museum of Natural History, which assigned two naturalists to the party. The group, with TR's son Kermit along, sailed from New York early in October and reached Rio de Janeiro late that month. Here, learning of a recent discovery of a long and unmapped river, called the River of Doubt, flowing northward toward the Amazon, TR abruptly scrapped his original plans. "We will go down that unknown river," he announced. Protests from friends and museum officials that this route was too dangerous did not deter him. "I have already lived and enjoyed as much of life as any other nine men I know," he said, "and if it be necessary for me to leave my remains in South America, I am quite ready to do so."

It took two months for them to hike to the headwaters of the River of Doubt. There the party, traveling in seven dugout canoes manned by sixteen boatmen, began to descend the river. How long it would take, or where they would come out, no one knew. It proved to be an agonizing ordeal that almost ended in tragedy, for the river was full of rapids and whirlpools. While trying to release two of the canoes that had become stuck between rocks, TR hurt his leg. The wound abscessed, and he developed a jungle fever. He carried on with the portage, however, straining his heart badly. Finally, with his strength gone, and expecting to die, he called Kermit to him and urged him to go ahead with the others, leaving him behind. He did not want to be a burden. Of course, they refused to do so. They had to carry him the rest of the way for he was too weak to help himself. Not until May 7, 1914, was he home again.

Science benefited greatly from that expedition. It placed a remote region of the Brazilian wilderness on the map, a river a thousand miles long, now called the Roosevelt. The two naturalists collected for the Museum of Natural History some 2,500 birds and 500 mammals, many hitherto unknown. This not to mention the many fishes, reptiles, insects, and amphibia they brought home.

But for TR himself it marked a sad change. His badly infected leg, together with lingering malaria and dysentery, sapped his strength permanently.

Three months after TR had settled in at Sagamore Hill a war broke out in Europe. A shot fired by a Serbian terrorist killed an Austrian archduke and set off a chain of reactions that shattered peace worldwide. It shocked people who had convinced themselves that civilization had reached the stage where disputes could be settled without resorting to arms. When the guns were fired, many Americans believed that the United States could and should stay out of the conflict in Europe. President Wilson at first tried to be neutral. He offered to help the warring nations restore peace.

But TR sided with the Allies and against Germany. Its invasion of Belgium and the atrocities charged against German

*TR stands beside wild game killed
during his 1913 Amazon safari.*

troops should be punished, and at once, he contended. When German submarines began sinking ships TR called Wilson's protests mild and feeble. And after the British passenger ship the *Lusitania* was sunk, with many American lives lost, TR wanted Wilson to break relations with Germany. Again TR's credo of "manliness," and the bloodletting needed to prove it, gripped him. He said that the young generation of Frenchmen and Englishmen had shown ugly traits, "and perhaps it was necessary that their manhood should be tried and purged in the ordeal of this dreadful fiery furnace."

So while Wilson moved slowly, partly because so much of his own party opposed going to war, TR kept putting the pressure on. He believed that if the Germans won the war, it would upset the balance of power in Europe and place America's security in danger. Enlarge the military, he urged, build up our armaments, wave the flag of patriotism! Anyone who sympathized with Germany, anyone who wanted the United States to remain neutral, anyone who took a pacifist position he called traitor, accusing such men of sabotage and sedition. He paraded himself as the 100 percent American, and his voice, often at the pitch of hysteria, demanded loyalty and obedience from all.

Like many in his time, TR held a black-and-white view of Americanism. He revived the old nativist intolerance that had plagued American politics in the past. He suspected the foreign-born of all sorts of terrible things and especially of radicalism. Wrote his biographer John Morton Blum: "He condoned mob action against labor radicals, pilloried those who strove to protect dissenters, fed the spirit that expressed itself in lynchings, amateur witch hunts, intolerance of every kind. Roosevelt was not alone in this. . . . But if he was not alone, he was also not often surpassed in his excursions into hate and paeans to conformity. . . . And he mixed his hateful talk with his awful cult of purging society by sacrifice in war. He disgraced not just his own, but his nation's reputation."

True to his own bellicose nature, he convinced himself that the nation's future would be safe only in his hands. So as

★

the Republican convention of 1916 approached, he maneuvered to have himself drafted as the Republican candidate for president. No one else would do, he told his friends. He failed to win the wide support needed. The Republicans nominated Charles Evans Hughes, a justice of the Supreme Court, instead. Hughes was defeated by Wilson, who ran on the enormously popular slogan: "He Kept Us Out of War."

Soon after the election, Wilson broke diplomatic relations with Germany, when it announced German submarines would attack any ship, including those from the United States, bound for Britain or France. On April 12, 1917, he asked Congress to declare war, pleading that "the world must be made safe for democracy." The majority in Congress voted for war, and the United States prepared to fight.

Expecting this, TR had made plans to play a dramatic role in combat. He wanted to organize a division of mounted infantrymen and to take his volunteers over to France to fight under his leadership. But after a meeting in the White House with TR, Wilson rejected the Roosevelt Division. Yes, TR was "a splendid man" and "a patriotic citizen," he said, but he was no military leader. "His experience in military life has been extremely short. He and many of the men with him are too old to render effective service, and in addition to that fact, he as well as others have shown intolerance of discipline."

World War I was no playground for the likes of Colonel Roosevelt's romantic Rough Riders. Facing poison gas and machine guns, what would they have done? Of course the aging and sickly TR would not accept that. Wilson's no infuriated him. The man was "purely a demagogue," "an utterly selfish and cold-blooded politician always." Nevertheless TR toured the country that fall, beating the drums for the war, rallying Americans to the flag. His own four sons volunteered, and the youngest, Quentin, a pilot, was killed in combat in July 1918, just before the war ended.

Somehow, TR could not cry. He thought he knew why Quentin had died. He wrote this to his son Archie: "Well, it is very dreadful, but, after all, he died as the heroes of old

*In this last photograph ever taken
of Teddy Roosevelt, he shares a
tender moment with his granddaughter.*

died; as brave and fearless men die when a great cause calls. If our country did not contain such men, it would not be our country."

Some 53,000 Americans died in that war. Another 230,000 were wounded. Even more died of disease, especially influenza.

The war ended in November 1918; TR himself lived only two months longer. In and out of hospitals in 1918, deaf in one ear, blind in one eye, crippled by attacks of rheumatism, he died in his sleep at Sagamore Hill on January 6, 1919. The immediate cause was a blood clot in his coronary artery. He was sixty.

Once again TR's name blazed in the headlines. The papers ran familiar pictures of him—hunting, riding, speechifying, strutting in his Rough Rider uniform. "America's best-loved citizen gone!" said one editorial. H.L. Mencken, the acid-tongued Baltimore journalist, said TR was "always gnawed by ambition and puerile vanities, and he died a disappointed and bitter man." If that was true, said his biographer Henry Pringle, the bitterness of his closing years "had come because he had climbed the heights too soon."

Wherever he went, he would continue to run things. On his first day in heaven, a story goes, he told Saint Peter: "Your choir is weak, inexcusably weak." So Saint Peter told him to take over that job. "Well," said TR, "I need ten thousand sopranos, ten thousand altos, and ten thousand tenors."

"But what about the basses?" asked Saint Peter.

"Oh," said TR, "I'll sing bass."

★   ★

A NOTE ON SOURCES

Trying to understand a life is always difficult: some say impossible. Your subject is human and therefore a collection of complexities and contradictions that defy easy analysis. You attempt to gather all the facts and then seek to make sense out of them. People change as they grow older, sometimes abruptly, sometimes gradually. I have tried to provide a portrait of Theodore Roosevelt that is coherent and meaningful. My own values—or prejudices, if you will—inevitably influence the outcome, for not everything your research comes up with can be fitted into a book of reasonable length. Selection must play a part, and that is where the biographer's personal point of view comes into play.

One way to begin to approach the subject is to read what your subject has to say about himself. When that subject is himself a prolific writer, as TR was, the task is formidable. Yet it produces only one side of the story. For TR, like anyone else, had his own view of himself and how he wished to present that self to the readers of his letters, his articles, his books, his diaries. Whether he is telling the truth, or consciously or unconsciously shading it to his own advantage, what you read needs to be checked against other sources.

First, then, the sources in his own words:

TR's letters were published in an eight-volume edition, *The Letters of Theodore Roosevelt*, ed. Elting E. Morison, Cambridge, Mass.: Harvard University Press, 1951–1954. Most of the 150,000 letters are in the Theodore Roosevelt Collection, Harvard College Library, Cambridge, Massachusetts. Diaries, journals, photographs, scrapbooks, and other mementos are also there. The large mass of TR's official papers and the correspondence to and from him are in the Theodore Roosevelt Papers, the Library of Congress, Washington, D.C.

Presidents sometimes publish autobiographies after they leave office. If they center on the years in the White House, readers buy them hoping to find hitherto undisclosed secrets as well as tasty tidbits about the personalities the great man dealt with. Too often such books are written with the help of others or even ghosted entirely by a professional author. This was not the case with *Theodore Roosevelt, An Autobiography*, New York: Da Capo, 1985. First issued in 1913, this is the highly original work of a veteran author whose ebullient ego stamps every page. There is much entertaining detail about his growing-up years and his adventures in the many political posts prior to the presidency. The book is just as significant for what it leaves out as for what it puts in.

The books TR wrote are collected in *The Works of Theodore Roosevelt*, National edition, New York: Scribner's, 1926. His early jottings of day-to-day activities and thoughts are in *Theodore Roosevelt's Diaries of Boyhood and Youth*, New York: Scribner's, 1928.

Biographies of TR include two extremely detailed, and therefore very useful ones that focus on his early life. Edmund Morris, *The Rise of Theodore Roosevelt*, New York: Ballantine, 1980, takes him up to the moment in 1901 when President McKinley was assassinated and TR, his vice president, replaced him. David McCullough, *Mornings on Horseback*, New York: Touchstone, 1982, carries the story to TR's second marriage, to Edith Carow, in 1886. The only recent complete biography is Nathan Miller, *Theodore Roosevelt: A Life*, New York: Morrow, 1992. This makes use of recently discovered new sources.

An earlier biography, Henry F. Pringle, *Theodore Roose-*

velt, San Diego: Harvest/HBJ, 1984, first published in 1931 and later revised, is a lively treatment by a veteran newspaperman that features the many controversies that swirled about TR's doings.

Studies of TR and his use of power that I found helpful include John Morton Blum, *The Republican Roosevelt*, Cambridge, Mass.: Harvard University Press, 1977; Howard K. Beale, *Theodore Roosevelt and the Rise of America to World Power*, Baltimore: Johns Hopkins Press, 1956; and Rhea Foster Dulles, *America's Rise to World Power*, New York: Harper, 1954. While TR's role in the Panama Canal episode is analyzed in these books, a more detailed account is offered in David McCullough, *The Path Between the Seas: The Creation of the Panama Canal, 1870–1914*, New York: Touchstone, 1977. To get a Latin American perspective on American intervention, I also used Hector Perez-Brignoli, *A Brief History of Central America*, Berkeley: University of California, 1989.

For the broad background against which TR's thrust for American expansion took place, I found these books useful: William Appleman Williams, *The Roots of the Modern American Empire*, New York: Random House, 1969; Bernard W. Weisberger, *Reaching for Empire, 1890–1901*, New York: Time, 1964; Sidney Lens, *The Forging of the American Empire*, New York: Crowell, 1971.

The rise of the giant corporations and the trusts with which TR contended is recorded in these histories: Ray Ginger, *Age of Excess: The U.S. from 1877 to 1914*. New York: Macmillan, 1965; Samuel P. Hays, *The Response to Industrialism, 1885–1914*, Chicago: University of Chicago Press, 1957; Olivier Zunz, *Making America Corporate: 1870–1920*, Chicago: University of Chicago Press, 1990; Naomi Lamoreaux, *The Great Merger Movement in American Business, 1895–1904*, New York; Cambridge University Press, 1985.

The reform movement that developed in response to corporate giantism is covered in many books. Among those I referred to are Richard Hofstadter, *The Age of Reform: From Bryan to FDR*, New York: Knopf, 1955; Eric Goldman, *Rendez-*

vous with Destiny: A History of Modern American Reform, New York: Knopf, 1952; Harold U. Faulkner, *Politics, Reform and Expansion, 1890–1900*, New York: Harper, 1959.

The protest movement of journalists and novelists is described in David M. Chalmers, *The Muckrake Years*, New York: Anvil, 1980. A broad sampling of the muckrakers' work is given in Harvey Swados, *Years of Conscience: The Muckrakers*, Cleveland: World, 1962. A fascinating account of the movement's origins combined with the personal story of its foremost writer is in *The Autobiography of Lincoln Steffens*, New York: Harcourt, 1931.

Race and racism figured prominently in the drive for American expansion and TR's thinking on that issue is assessed in several studies: Two titles deal with the Brownsville incident: John D Weaver, *The Brownsville Raid*, New York: Norton, 1970, and Ann J. Lane, *The Brownsville Affair*, New York: 1971. TR's ideas about African-Americans, Native Americans, immigration, and imperialism are analyzed in Thomas G. Dyer, *Theodore Roosevelt and the Idea of Race*, Baton Rouge: Louisiana State University Press, 1980, and in Richard Drinnon, *Facing West: The Metaphysics of Indian-Hating and Empire Building*. New York: Schocken, 1990.

For TR as conservationist I relied on Paul R. Cutright, *Theodore Roosevelt: The Making of a Conservationist*, Urbana: University of Illinois Press, 1985. Insight into TR's second marriage and the role of his First Lady is found in Sylvia Jukes Morris, *Edith Kermit Roosevelt*, New York: Vintage, 1990.

Wherever possible I have listed paperback editions.

Beyond the written record, it helps to get the feeling of a historic figure by visiting the places linked closely to his or her life. Luckily there are two such sites where TR lived; both are in or near New York City.

The Theodore Roosevelt Birthplace is at 28 East Twentieth Street in Manhattan. It is administered by the National Park Service in cooperation with the Theodore Roosevelt Association. The original house was demolished in 1916, but after TR's death in 1919, the site was purchased and TR's boyhood home was reconstructed as a memorial. The rooms have been restored to their appearance at the time of TR's childhood. The family moved out when he was fourteen. For information on visiting hours or to arrange group visits call (212) 260-1616.

Sagamore Hill, built by TR in 1884–1885, was his home for the rest of his life, some thirty years. It is a twenty-three-room Victorian house of frame and brick. Today it looks much as it did some seventy-five years ago. The furnishings consist of the original Roosevelt pieces, with objects the family loved and used in every room. The house looks out over Oyster Bay Harbor and Long Island Sound. It is now a national historic site administered by the National Park Service. It can be reached easily by Long Island Railroad or by car. For visiting hours call (516) 922-1221.

INDEX

★

★ ★

ABOUT THE AUTHOR

Milton Meltzer has published over eighty-five books for young people and adults in the fields of history, biography, and social issues, and has also dealt with such diverse topics as memory, names, the potato, and gold. He has written or edited for newspapers, magazines, books, radio, television, and films.

The Theodore Roosevelt life is the latest of many biographies, which include such subjects as Andrew Jackson, Jefferson, Washington, Franklin, Lincoln, Thoreau, Mark Twain, Langston Hughes, Mary McLeod Bethune, and Dorothea Lange.

Among the many honors for his books are five nominations for the National Book Award as well as the Christopher, Jane Addams, Carter G. Woodson, Jefferson Cup, Washington Book Guild, Olive Branch, and Golden Kite awards. Many of his books have been chosen for the honor lists of the American Library Association, the National Council of Teachers of English and the National Council for the Social Studies, as well as for the *New York Times* Best Books of the Year list.

Meltzer and his wife, Hildy, live in New York City. They have two daughters, Jane and Amy, and two grandsons, Benjamin and Zachary. Mr. Meltzer is a member of the Authors Guild, American PEN, and the Organization of American Historians.